Welcome to Lizard Motel

Children, Stories, and the Mystery of Making Things Up

A MEMOIR

Barbara Feinberg

Beacon Press
BOSTON

Beacon Press
25 Beacon Street
Boston, Massachusetts 02108-2892
www.beacon.org

Beacon Press books
are published under the auspices of
the Unitarian Universalist Association of Congregations.

Printed in the United States of America

07 06 05 04   8 7 6 5 4 3 2 1

This book is printed on acid-free paper that meets the uncoated paper ANSI/NISO specifications for permanence as revised in 1992.

Text design by Dean Bornstein
Composition by Wilsted and Taylor Publishing Services

Library of Congress Cataloging-in-Publication Data
Feinberg, Barbara.
Welcome to Lizard Motel : children, stories, and the mystery of making things up : a memoir / Barbara Feinberg.
p. cm.
Includes bibliographical references and index.
ISBN 0-8070-7144-7 (cloth : alk. paper)
1. Children—Books and reading—United States. 2. Imagination in children. 3. Home and school—United States. 4. Reading—Parent participation—United States. 5. Feinberg, Barbara. I. Title.
Z1037.A1F45 2004
028.5'5—dc22   2004000710

Note to the Reader: *I have changed the names of some children described. The children I write about are real people, however, and are not composite portraits. Information about works cited in* Welcome to Lizard Motel *can be found in the section "Notes and Further Thoughts," at the back of the book.*

TO DAN

There is a special period of … childhood, approximately from five or six to eleven or twelve—between the strivings of animal infancy and the storms of adolescence—when the natural world is experienced in some highly evocative way, producing in the child a sense of some profound continuity with the natural processes and presenting overt evidence of a biological basis of intuition. … It is principally to this middle age range in their early life that writers say they return in memory in order to renew the power and impulse to create.

— Edith Cobb

Chapter One

The day started out all right. I woke early and, still in my nightgown, walked out to the porch and began to paint the walls. I had never planned on doing this. The porch didn't need to be painted, and because of all its windows and high ceiling—not to mention the bicycles and muddy shoes and old couches that needed to be shoved aside—to paint it was a huge undertaking, one I never would have wanted to do. I must have woken from a dream in which painting the porch was occurring, because as I found myself prying off the lid of a leftover can of yellow paint and sinking a brush in, I felt perfect equanimity, as if I were merely continuing a project, rather than launching a new one.

The porch is enclosed with windows. Two face into the interior of the house; three walls are lined entirely with long windows that open outward, to the garden, as in a Danish farmhouse. Each is composed of many small panes of thick glass. Through the pocked glass, on this morning, the sky was heavy with pending rain, and the tips of tall white flowers peered in. Perhaps due to some remnant of the same dream, I had the feeling of seeing the garden from the portals of a boat, as if stretching beyond were not garden and stone but a calm, early morning sea, only just beginning to undulate from an oncoming storm, which for the moment was still in the distance. Birds dove below my line of vision. I sank the brush deep to its shoulders, and stroked the excess off with two or three flops. Each time I slathered yellow on the wall, a path of lit water seemed to open.

My children ambled in. Alex is twelve, very tall, and has bright blue eyes. Clair is seven, round and dark, and her hair was tangled from sleep. They were quiet and sleepy. They lay down on an old couch. After a while of resting and watching me, they decided they wanted to paint too, and I found two more brushes, although one was only a little eyeliner brush. We opened cans of paint, left over from other projects. Due to our lax housekeeping habits, the cans had never been put away and had been standing on the porch for a long time.

"Let's paint whatever we want," I said. Clair made white and pink daisies along the windowsill. Alex painted a window frame the same grey-blue as the sky, and using the eyeliner brush, made tiny yellow dots, like hopeful lights. "Dad likes flowers," Clair said. While we chatted, the feeling of being in the middle of water persisted, and when I mentioned it, my kids nodded. The porch was a floating houseboat, the odds and ends and muddy shoes merely stuff we had heaped on board. When the wind threw the windows open, their ancient latches creaking, we held on to whatever we could grab, as if we were on the high seas.

After a while, Alex announced to Clair in a serious voice, "We have to do that thing," and she, delighted to be needed by her older brother, nodded, and they bade me goodbye, took their brushes inside to wash, and trooped off into the house.

I climbed up on the arm of the couch and, having found a can called "Summer Blue," began painting the trim of the large window that looks from the porch into the living room. When my children came back into the living room, they walked into the blue frame. They had changed out of their pajamas, and looked as if they were getting ready to go to work, which it turned out was sort of the case. My daughter was wearing a little vest over her T-shirt.

I couldn't hear them, but could see that they were clearly discussing an audiotape Alex was holding, a novel on tape he'd gotten from the library the day before. The book, I knew, was *Chasing Redbird* by Sharon Creech; this was the book he was supposed to read over the summer, in preparation for seventh grade. And he dreaded this. He had read another book by Sharon Creech for the previous summer's assigned reading, and hated that, said it was too "dark." So this summer, he'd settled on the idea of listening to *Chasing Redbird* instead of reading it. This way, he'd reasoned, he could have the company of his sister, and this would make the experience more "bearable."

I watched as they put the tape in the cassette slot. They were sitting side by side on the couch. I tapped on the glass, but they were engrossed now, waiting for it to begin. I was reminded of how the poet Pablo Neruda described tiptoeing to his parents to show them his first poem, but they "were immersed in one of those hushed conversations that, more than a river, separate the world of children and the world of grownups."

A woman's voice came on. I could not make out her

words, but the volume was high, and the feeling and quality of her voice permeated the glass. It was a low voice, with no lift or variation.

"Ah, a sad story," I thought happily. Alex and Clair had spent the summer roaming around, reading *Harry Potter*, playing, swimming, and lounging. Alex had read a gamut of scripts and biographies of comedians. This foray into a sad tale sounded intriguing now, on this dark morning; it seemed important, more akin to "serious literature." I imagined a little alcove, isolated but protected from wind by rocks. Sadness in books was often beautiful, or poignant. I painted and thought of the book *The Snow Goose* by Paul Gallico, which I barely remembered, save for the spare print and the windswept landscape, undercut with a feeling of loss. I thought of the book *The Victim* by Saul Bellow, *The Ballad of the Sad Café* by Carson McCullers. I knew my children were not listening to any of these, but they were the books that came to mind.

The voice on the tape continued, shaking the walls with its sad thunder, and I suddenly wondered if I was making a mistake, painting the porch these summery colors. It got so cold in here when the weather turned. There was no heat, and these windows, no matter how tightly bolted, flew open in the wilder winds, which thrashed hats, gloves, and old newspapers. The porch was the last place to get through before one was safely inside. Shouldn't it be left as a simple passing-through room, to be exited as quickly as possible? I imagined the bleak sky, the "stale" grass, as Clair once described winter grass, rolling beyond the windows. Would this room be comforting to enter then? What does one want in winter? Great majestic red? Would these dreamy colors feel annoying? Or insubstantial, a child offering only a thin cardigan?

The terrible voice on the tape—it had become a drone—suddenly shut off; I had my brush poised in midair. The silence was pure relief. My children were now standing, and I watched as Alex gave one curt nod to Clair, and at that signal, they both proceeded to march, elbows bent, in a tight circle. They stopped abruptly, and did five or six deep knee bends. They looked as if they were in an old Jack LaLanne commercial. I knew they probably had some sense of comedy about acting like this, taking an allotted exercise break—their sense of the absurd was in full swing. But when they sat down again, and Alex switched on the audio, and the drone commenced, they looked tense, not giggly, and the phrase "bracing themselves" came to mind.

What exactly was this book? Aside from the title, I knew nothing about it. In fact, all the books Alex was assigned in school were foreign to me. I recalled his last year's language arts teacher, on Back to School Night. I had been excited to meet her, because Alex adored her and her class. She was a graceful young woman, in a cream pants suit—a new teacher, hip, brimming with enthusiasm. "A delight," she'd said of Alex as we shook hands.

But now I remembered that I had felt a slight wariness with regard to the school's choice of books. I remembered her gesturing to the paperbacks the class would be reading. "Most of these books are recommended by the American Library Association, and many are Newbery prize winners." The books were propped around the room. They all had teens on the covers. I didn't recognize a single title. I had picked up one and read that it promised "profound struggle." I put it back carefully.

The good warm feeling in the room had persisted. When the teacher cited an experience she'd had the previous year, during which a mother "came up to me and said, 'Gee, thanks a lot, my daughter was up all night crying because of the death of a whale in that book'" (it wasn't *Moby-Dick*), we all laughed a bit at the sarcasm, and from a certain happiness we felt at the idea of a child being so swept up in a story. But now I remembered something else that had been said: "You see," the teacher had gone on to explain, "A good book should make you cry."

These words came back to me as I watched my children now. They were sitting so stiffly, their spines arched. Their posture was the opposite of how they sat when they were absorbed. Why, exactly, did school want them to cry?

I had seen Alex like this many times during the year, when I'd passed his room in the evening; he always left his door open. There he'd be, reading one or another book assigned from school, under the cone of his desk lamp. He never looked at ease while he read. I had tried adjusting his light, and suggested he close his door. No, he always wanted the door open when he read, didn't like to be alone with these books. "Everyone dies in them," he told me wearily. He'd recited the litany: a story about a town besieged by radioactive poisoning; one in which a girl searches for her mother, only to find her mother has committed suicide; children being abused in foster care, never told why their mothers weren't coming back. The list went on.

It can't be that bad, I always thought; reading, after all, is good. His teacher was a fine captain; I trusted her sense of direction. (But the choice of books?) I had never offered too much sympathy. Once or twice I'd picked up a book and studied the cover, where a photograph of a teen stared back at me, challengingly, such that I always lowered my eyes. Once in a while I had put my hand on Alex's shoulder and, wondering what to say, found only these words: "Just do it."

What had I meant? I meant it in the same way someone might have once said, "Just drink your milk," or "Just take your cod liver oil," or, I realized suddenly, the way someone might believe that a child ought to endure a beating, because even though it hurt, it was a "good beating," would make him better, build character.

Was this kind of reading akin to a "good beating?"

Would the monotony of the voice break? I was listening for a shift in tone, a ravine of mystery, but no shift came. I realized no change would come. I had been listening for a certain music of sadness; instead, these were the brittle and fatty sounds of heavy depression. The voice was aggressive too, the way depression can make someone hostile.

"You know nothing about how bad life really is," it seemed to be droning. "You need this big dose of reality I am giving you. It's killing me, this talking, but I'm doing it for you."

Alex and Clair looked drained, and tired. What dour and horrible future were they boning up on? I thought of banging on the glass with my fists. I wanted to yell, "Come out!" I wanted to yell, "You won't have to go it alone like the kids in those books! That isn't literature! That isn't life! Step back in the flow!" I saw my reflection: Mother in her nightgown, balancing on a getaway gondola with a paintbrush. I wanted to cry, "What crazy modern port have we landed in?"

Chapter Two

It is easy to spot Alex's assigned reading books among his real books. His real books are worn, and cling to a driving force, namely Comedy. These books are stacked and bulging in his shelves, all the novels by Louis Sachar, Daniel Pinkwater, Barbara Park. And then thicker books—the biographies of Milton Berle, Sid Caesar, Larry Gelbart; all the scripts from *Our Show of Shows;* the script of *A Funny Thing Happened on the Way to the Forum;* a book called *170 Years of Show Business.* But mostly his library serves to illuminate and honor Mel Brooks, his hero.

Alex was in the second grade when he first saw Mel; it was on a television talk show where Mel chatted with other comedians and writers, but Alex was drawn intently, exclusively, to Mel. (Later he told us it was because he thought Mel was the "free-est.") We were sitting in the living room eating Chinese food when, after the opening wacky moments, Alex rose to his feet, as if he were in the presence of a transformative celestial vision that was calling his name. He did not sit again during the show, and in a sense, he has not sat since.

Everything Mel Brooks has ever written, directed, acted in, claims to have read (e.g., *She Stoops to Conquer* by Oliver Goldsmith) has been studied; any actor ever to have been in one of his productions (Anne Bancroft, Madeline Kahn), or to have written with him, has been researched and their biographies and artistic careers pursued. A picture of Mel, laughing, big-nosed, hangs over Alex's bed. From this epicenter of Mel, Alex has gradually broadened his interests over time to include a range of plays, especially Neil Simon's, scripts in general—most of them in pale blue covers from the Drama Bookshop—and the lives and works of other directors and comedians.

Among these worn texts, the school-issued books seem sleek and untouched in comparison. They are paperbacks, moderate in length, and on their covers are drawings of slim, attractive teenagers. The drawings are so hyper-real that I have to study them for a moment to confirm that they are not photographs. The teens are looking straight at me, some with their arms crossed across their chests. They look cool, defiant; they manage to look at me but not seem exposed. I never read any of these books in my own childhood (nothing in this pile was published before 1972). Who are these bold teenage protagonists? Do these books constitute a new kind of book, represent a new sensibility with regard to children? What, beyond the weird drone I heard through the wall, is the nature of their grimness?

I pluck out two at random and bring them downstairs. I decide to read *Walk Two Moons,* by Sharon Creech, a book I know Alex had to read last summer, before entering sixth grade. It has a girl on the cover, although we can see only her long flowing hair. She is turned toward an intriguing landscape of purple mountains and clear water, with a vibrant sunset beyond the mountains. Stamped in the middle of the cover, as if it were a moon floating in that clear water, is the golden seal of a Newbery medal.

I sit in a slatted chair, out on my front lawn, alone for a few hours, since my children are at the town pool and my husband won't be home until dinnertime. The metal legs of the chair sink into the earth when I sit, and I have to adjust the chair several times to get it to stay level. A white picket fence encircles my yard. I begin to read. I can see my neighbors walk by, and they have only to peer over the fence and there I am, stretched out, but I harbor a sense of privacy nonetheless.

The book is about Salamanca, a girl whose mother has strangely and abruptly left home; Sal travels across the country with her grandparents looking for her. The plan is to show up where she thinks her mother has gone, on her mother's birthday, and coax her to return. The story is told by Sal, and takes place mostly in the car, in dialogue between Sal and her two interesting and unusual grandparents. She spends much time telling fascinating stories about things that have been happening to her since her mother has gone. I set about reading *Walk Two Moons* with the notion of keeping an analytic distance, but the story draws me in, and I begin to read slowly to savor the language. The writing is lyrical, the insights of the narrator sensitively revealed. I put the book down midway for a break with a feeling of pleasant surprise. I feel excited for my son: here is an ambitious book, ambitious not only in terms of the writer's reach, but also in the way that it calls upon the young reader to stretch his way of hearing a story and seeing a world.

I walk to the town pool to find my kids. While I walk, I have that heightened sense of my surroundings—of leaves and shadows for example—that comes from having been under the spell of an observant narrator.

"Ma!" Alex calls when he sees me. "Watch me swim." I watch him swim gracefully across the pool. "How did I look?"

"Great."

"But did you watch me?"

"Yes, you're a beautiful swimmer." I crouch down at the edge of the pool. "What should I read next?" I say. "I'm almost done with *Walk Two Moons.*"

He looks shocked. "Why are you reading that?"

"It's actually—" I want to say "good," but something tells me to modify this—"not so bad, I mean I expected worse."

"It's bad," he assures me. "And please don't talk to me about those books." Then he whispers in a sharp way, "Go away! Don't remind me about school."

Other boys swim over, eleven or twelve years old, some chubby, some very skinny, all hanging onto the ledge. Water glistens on their faces as they look up at me. I have known the lot since nursery school. I decide to address them all. "I'm reading *Walk Two Moons,*" I say. "When I'm done I'm gonna want to read some other books you guys read last year in school. Do you remember any titles? Any of them good?"

They stare at me in wonderment that I should be reading schoolbooks in the summer. They are tilting their heads, trying to square this piece of oddness with what they know about me as a basically rational person. But they are too polite to go on about this, and are, all told, helpful fellows. They come up with titles. They consider that the book they had to read this summer, *Chasing Redbird,* also by Sharon Creech—the one Alex had been listening to on tape—was "all right."

"Just all right."

"Actually pretty bad."

"No, not that bad."

Other titles: *Rising Phoenix* ("that's about radioactive poisoning"), *Bridge to Terabithia.* "It's good," a boy says, "but it might make you a little too sad."

"I hated that," another says.

"You want to really feel sad?" an older boy asks me, suddenly seeming to have figured out that this is my goal.

"Well not necessarily—" I begin.

But he speaks with authority: "Read *They Cage the Animals at Night.* That's the saddest. It's about a boy who was an orphan, and then the man who wrote it came to our school and told us what it was like to be an orphan." We are silent for a moment while we think about this. I can see their legs under the water, drifting idly.

After a while, Alex says, "*Harry Potter*'s the best." This is a self-evident truth among the group, so obvious that no one needs to add to it. A long discussion about the most recent *Harry Potter* ensues, and the mood lightens. Then two girls, also eleven or twelve, who have been listening nearby, come over to offer their opinions. They speak to me, since it is the habit of these boys and girls to generally ignore each other.

"You were saying something about Sharon Creech?" says one, as if mentioning a girl in her grade. A look of absolute disdain crosses her freckly face. "Oh, she thinks she's such a nature girl."

While I ponder this, not quite sure what she means, the other girl, in the same sickened tone, adds a comment that also seems significant, but in what way I am not yet sure. "Sharon Creech thinks we're the lowest form of life."

I walk home. The sun is high overhead, but a late August wind is stirring the garden. Wild shadows roll across the grass. I sit back down in my slatted lawn chair and carefully pick up *Walk Two Moons*. I resume reading. It is still engrossing, although increasingly upsetting things begin to pile up. We learn about the bloody miscarriage and hysterectomy Sal's mother endured before she deserted her family. Sal's grandmother has a stroke and must go to the hospital. The grandfather must remain to watch over her, so Sal drives on to find her mother by herself. She arrives in the town her mother has fled to, and yes, she has made it right on her mother's birthday. I am excited, the long journey has come to an end (the reader is told that Sal's grandmother has died in the meantime, but for the moment the girl does not know this), and I cannot wait for the mother and daughter to hold each other in their arms. Only it turns out the mother is not there, since she's been dead all along. She was killed in a bus accident. We find this out in the last pages. There are some hasty resolutions afterwards, but these feel tacked on and don't do much to dispel the book's great bad wallop of an ending.

I am stunned by this death and all this sudden cramming in of dismal facts. I feel as if I've been had, the way you might feel if, all along, you thought someone was your friend, only to find he is a paid actor. The ending, and suddenly the whole book, feel immeasurably contrived, weighted with a huge message—something about growing up and having to leave one's mother behind. About having to rely on yourself. Something like that. What had begun as a real book, sad yes, but complex and original, has ended as a tearjerker.

I go inside and eat lunch and pace through the house. Then in late afternoon, I pick up *Bridge to Terabithia* by Katherine Paterson. The cover of the book features two teens, or possibly preteens, a boy standing under a great tree, and a girl sitting on a rock, also in the shelter of the great tree. Why they might be under such a vast tree together is unclear, since she is reading a book, in a tentative posture that makes her seem just a tad ethereal, a tad visionlike; and he is staring off into the distance in a way that telegraphs to me (granted, perhaps, in my suspicious condition) depression or loneliness, something painful. *Bridge to Terabithia,* like *Walk Two Moons,* is stamped with the gold Newbery medal.

Wary as I am, I begin, and as with the previous book, am quickly pulled in. The writing of this book is very beautiful, impressively so, and feels deeply inhabited by the main character, who turns out to be the boy, named Jess. He is ten. He lives in rural Tennessee with his family, who are poor and overburdened, and not sensitive to their artistic son. While the book is told in the third person, the narrator is intimately aligned with the boy, and reserves no asides, no perceptions apart from his.

The story centers on the evolving friendship between

Jess and a new girl, Leslie, who moves to Tennessee from up North. She is different from anyone Jess has known. She has a rich imagination, is educated, has academic, unconventional, wise parents. Together Jess and Leslie build an imaginary palace in the woods; they rig up a rope swing to cross the lovely little creek; they play in the shadows. They call their kingdom Terabithia. Gradually Jess's habitual shyness diminishes, as he feels understood by his new, wise friend. I read slowly because the writing is so good. My good faith is restored. The writing has an unflinching quality; it is so accurate about the way something feels, and how life is experienced, that I feel neither shielded nor hustled, but on the brink of really living this boy's life with him. Time slows, like watching a bee in the air. I turn the pages slowly.

But then, as the sun begins to sink, my children are at the gate, exhausted and radiant from a day in the water, and my thighs are creviced with deep indentations from the slats on the lawn chair, it happens again: I reach the penultimate chapter, and one of the children (Leslie) is suddenly killed. It happens while Jess is off to his first art museum with a beloved schoolteacher. "Your girlfriend got killed," his sister cries when he comes home at the end of that lovely day. Leslie had been swinging on that rope, and the rope broke. It is speculated that she must have hit her head and drowned. I hear myself moan, "Oh no," partly because three deaths in one afternoon are more than I can take.

But this death feels worse than the other ones. I read about how stunned Jess feels. He is numb. He gets up the next morning and eats pancakes and doesn't remember that Leslie is dead, and has to be retold. Jess's grief is delicately described, in the same unflinching detail as was his earlier flowering. But as I read every word, I notice something changing in me. I am not "in" the story anymore. I am not reading to drink in the life of the book, I am not stretched out across my languid chair. I've been woken up from the dream of the book, and now I sit tense and hunched over; while I still sort of care about how Jess will manage, I stand outside of the book and coldly weigh each word.

I think of the author, Katherine Paterson, for the first time. Why in the world did you kill off your character? To make a point? I berate her: You didn't set the death up right. You didn't prepare us. On some level we have to be prepared. I wasn't aware, even subliminally, of a dark forewarning; no haunting undertone. This was a complete shock. Even a shock should reverberate somehow. An ending should be a manifestation, should have a feeling of necessity to it. Your book posed no question, even unconsciously, that this death answers. Random and artificially constructed. Cooked up to make a point. But what point?

But even as a fed-up literary critic, I still read slowly, carefully searching each sentence, as if combing through debris for something lost, not willing to let this beautiful book just fall apart.

But there are so few pages left now that Leslie is dead. The death was what we were hurtling toward all along, even though we had no clue; we were lulled into thinking we had all the time we needed. But since the drama is over, the book has not much more to say. One more week is spent looking in at Jess, and by week's end we are told he is feeling a bit better. His family tries to be more thoughtful, and even his teacher, who had been remote, reaches out to him. But as I say, it all happens in just a few pages. Jess goes back to the woods where he and Leslie used to play Terabithia. The story is quickly ending.

Then I come upon these paragraphs, and I know I am being told something important:

> It occurred to [Jess] that perhaps Terabithia was a castle where you came to be knighted. After you stayed for a while and grew strong you had to move on. For hadn't Leslie, even in Terabithia, tried to push back the walls of his mind and make him see beyond the shining world—huge and terrible and beautiful and very fragile? . . .
>
> Now it was time for him to move out. She wasn't there, so he must go for both of them. It was up to him to pay back to the world in beauty and caring what Leslie had loaned him in vision and strength.

"The Meaning" is being offered here—an explanation, a way to view all that's happened. This realistic book, it seems, is meant to be viewed as a parable, whose components I can imagine written on a blackboard:

Terabithia = Childhood Imagination

Childhood Imagination = Personal Strength

BUT

Terabithia/Childhood Imagination must ultimately be forfeited.

I drop the book on the grass and close my eyes.

I feel unsettled. What's wrong? I feel like a child, as if something bad has happened. I am longing for comfort. It is as if I am standing with my ear to the wall trying to make out words muttered from a distant part of the house, barely audible. And then the words I make out are so abstract —"caring," "vision," "strength"—they are not worth the trouble. These are not the words I want. I preferred that other way of talking: when time stood still, like watching a bee.

Why has this book left me feeling so unconsoled?

Evening is coming on. The white fence has taken on a blue glow, as if it alone is absorbing the draining light.

I am a lump in the lawn chair. I can hear the TV on in my house, distantly. I picture my children sunk on the couch in their wet bathing suits. I think of marching in and saying, "Hey, change into dry clothes!" But I don't move. I am drained from reading too long in the sun. My face feels sore, as if I've gotten a sunburn.

But around me, the trees are roused; they have grown dark, as if they are now one huge presence against the pink sky. The wind is near, and then very far, more like an echo, and the dusk takes on a deeper dimension, beyond the small planet of my yard. Autumn is approaching. Soon Alex will disappear down the path on the side of the house each morning to school.

He used to hesitate before he left, when he was younger,

when he first started middle school. "Sometimes I miss you in the day," he told me. I picture myself standing out here, seeing him off in the early morning. My husband would have left for work already, and our neighbors were mostly gone too, so we were more or less alone, which was good because there I was standing out in the street in my nightgown and slippers. Didn't I sing to him as he descended? A tuneless, nonsensical chant, left over from when he was a toddler:

walking walking
always walking
walking walking
all day long.

We both knew the scene was kind of funny, absurd. But I remember asking him, "Should I stop?" and him calling back, "Just keep singing it, but not so loud." So I sang it until the trees swallowed him and I couldn't see him.

Now he is not so tentative. Every night before school, he will do his homework, diligently, pack his own things up, manage projects: he is masterful in his realm. When he leaves down the steps, his blue knapsack will look heavy and lumpy, but he's not dwarfed by it. Sometimes he will say goodbye a few times; he hugs me, a hard hug, resting his head on my shoulder, over before I know it. But once he's out the door he won't turn around again. If I ask him something then, he'll call his answer backward, but not even slow down, as if once he's set his compass he must proceed. His stride is purposeful. He looks like "a youth just starting out."

What does someone just starting out in the world need to take? If I were to stand in the street in my slippers and call after him now that he is twelve, as he descends the steps, what would I call?

"Be brave." ?

"Seek adventure!" ?

("Come home at three." ?)

What book in his knapsack might help him along his way? (Not the two I've read today; they seem too nerve-racking, freighted with anxiety. They would weigh him down.)

From my half-opened eyes the sun is reflected in the chrome on the car. The sinking sun has lit rainwater deep in the crevices of rocks, making the crevices look as if they are filled with gold ink. Everywhere there is spangling; there are blinding surfaces.

Who was I when I was eleven and twelve? I picture my young, smooth face peering amiably back from photographs. Dark hair, a headband. But the thought of being eleven has always conjured this image: a sketch of a girl in chalk. Maybe, out on the sidewalk, drawing, playing hopscotch, I once tried to outline my own shadow in chalk, then stepped away and saw how vaporous and distorted my outlined shadow looked.

My body felt too light. Something felt missing. But at the same time I must have looked "ready." I was approached by older boys. By men. But to myself, I was a person within a person, and the person within had misplaced something, and had to find it.

And at eleven I lost my ability to draw. It seemed to

happen on one day, although it probably was a succession of days. I had drawn and painted since I was very small, had planned to be a painter when I grew up. Crayons were characters in their stadium of a box, and I had key players: magenta, burnt sienna, gold. When I lifted the lid of the crayon box every morning, I oriented myself by these three, like finding my family in a crowded room.

And then abruptly, or so it seemed, I got up one morning to draw but found that the page had closed off, perhaps sometime during the night. I drew a line, but the paper was bolted, and rejected the line, so the line stayed on the surface. Nothing was in motion anymore. I tried again and again, but after that first bad day, nothing moved, and I forever ended up with the same picture: a drawing divided in half by a gash I never remembered making: two distinct pictures. I had no desire to complete either one, so I gave up.

One Saturday when it was raining, and I had been roaming around my house, I asked my father to recommend a book for me, and he came back some time later, after having given it obvious careful thought. It turned out to be just the right book for me: a battered copy of *A Tree Grows in Brooklyn* by Betty Smith.

I picture myself on my bed, curled around the book, or sitting up, my mouth dry from nerves. I was in the world of Brooklyn, which was so remarkably like my streets in New York City, and Francie was eleven just like me, and she walked through her neighborhood and noticed the secret things I noticed. Up until these pages, I never imagined that anyone else thought about such things: the faces and hands of shopkeepers, the personality of candy, the interesting way coins felt in your hand. Francie was alone like me, but in some way she wasn't lonely; nor was I, really: we shared a kind of pioneer quality, drinking in life beyond our own small apartments. She loved her father most of all, her father who was an alcoholic, although no such word was used in the book. We only knew how he acted when he drank, and when he was sleeping it off, and how kind and grand he was toward his daughter, and how drawn-in and bitter his wife was. Through these descriptions we came to know the presence of alcohol. I was guided along the landscape of this family life by the narrator, who was alert and wise, and never skipped over what we (Francie and I) felt. Through this widening, clear lens, I glimpsed my own life, and the presence of alcohol in my family too, even though in my house the bottles were kept hidden. And the immensity of love, the tragedy intertwined with the love a daughter has toward a doomed father, and the love—but scary, unacknowledged dread, too—toward a mother.

Sometimes I would close the book and stare at the name of the author, Betty Smith. I did not like that her name was on the cover of the book, because its presence was a reminder that the book wasn't real, and had been made by one, mere person. I preferred to think only of the narrator, who was keen and generous, somehow, and of all the characters, whom I felt I knew. When I closed the book for the night, I trained myself to avert my eyes from the author's name.

How was this book, with all its reality and sadness, different from the two I'd read today?

When Francie's father died, something in me collapsed.

It set off dreams of my own father in a coffin; the dreams persisted for years. It must have given form to feelings that had been floating in me previously, but up until the moment of reading the feelings had been underground, lurking. Suddenly the prospect of a father dying—my father —came clearly to mind. It became an obsessive worry. I remember lying curled on my bed, crying so hard I felt my face turn inside out. What if I were left, like Francie, with only a bitter mother? For the first time, I thought consciously about the "future" and the prospect of a life that would inevitably include loss. I bit the fleshy part of my arm for comfort. But whom could I turn to? I spoke to no one about this experience. If I had tried to explain why I couldn't stop crying, what could anyone have said? How can anyone offer comfort about the death of a character in a book?

And yet there was something full about it all, brimming, exciting, alluring. The book was bigger than the tragedy; it was close and protective in that world, as well as tragic. Aunt Sissy, for example, who gave Francie shiny pennies as a gift; the kindness and ingenuity of this episode has stayed with me all these years. The book portrayed a whole life, not just one driven by a "problem." The death occurred in the middle of the book, not at the end like the deaths in *Walk Two Moons* and *Bridge to Terabithia*. Francie's father's death was followed by the chronicling of her ongoing experiences, as she picked up the pieces and found some peace, so that her life widened again.

The book created a dome around itself, and I felt enclosed

within it. The truth was that I liked the privacy of the enclosed story. The book invited me in. Each word felt just for me, to me. In fact, I didn't feel the need or desire to talk about it. The book was a house; we lived in it together. Betty Smith was with me. We all knew how we felt.

Maybe this is what made *A Tree Grows in Brooklyn* such an intimate, deepening, experience, while *Bridge to Terabithia* left me cold and sad. I don't know if *A Tree Grows in Brooklyn* would hold up for me now. But I do know that if I had read *Bridge to Terabithia* then, when I was young, I would have been mostly upset by it, left jittery.

Sitting here in the darkening yard, watching the wind stir the puddles, I think of my younger self.

"Childhood is the well of being," Bachelard wrote. He describes a child first glimpsing his reflection in such a well:

> Already in his image living beneath the earth, the child does not recognize himself. A mist is on the water; plants which are too green frame the mirror. A cold blast breathes in the depths. The face which comes back in this night of the earth is a face from another world.

I am remembering Alex on a night early this summer. He, Clair, my husband, Dan, and I were in the park. It was a beautiful night, but we were not having fun. Alex was irritable. We had gone to the park, in fact, to try to cheer him up.

It was a moonless night; the field was vast and empty, lit only with discrete pools of light from lone streetlamps. We were playing tag. Under the lights, the grass was bright green. Beyond, in the field, flowers and bushes were awake, lush, stirred slightly by breezes. There was a sense of color buried under black. Maybe this prompted Clair to call out across the field, "Daddy, do you think everybody sees green the same way?"

I heard Dan reply, "Well, this is a good question. I wonder about it too." And then a conversation ensued, a rather intellectual one, drawn from his interest in philosophy. "One man," he said, "whose name was Bishop Berkeley, wondered if there is really such a thing as green at all in the world, or if our brains are just making up the whole idea of green."

"Tell her about 'objective' and 'subjective,'" I called out, my voice echoing through the dark.

But maybe from memory of my own fragility when I was young, I had a bad premonition suddenly, as if someone weak, or very tired, was trying to keep his balance on a rough sea. Sure enough, when I looked for Alex, he had vanished. I searched for him, quietly, and found him behind a hedge. I could see him in the partial light of a streetlamp, and he was crying. When I asked him what was wrong, he whispered, "Everything is changing."

"What's changing?"

"Everything."

I reached out to touch him, but he receded farther into the shadows.

"I love you," I said. "What's the matter? Everything is OK."

"You don't know anything."

"Tell me."

"I can't."

"Try. Try to put it into words."

Beyond, Dan and Clair were playing with a dog who had trotted up, and the shadow of its tail was flipping across the field. The flipping emphasized how wide and free the field was. Just a few months back, Alex would have dived into this lush darkness. But now he just stayed behind the streetlamp, as if the night in front of him were too vast to enter.

Finally, in a voice so low I had to ask him to repeat it, he said, "If no one sees green the same, what's the point?"

This did seem like a central question: I took it to mean that if we are all going it alone, how could life be good? Something like that. I opened my mouth to speak, but I had no idea what to say, what he meant exactly, what was required of me. Actually I had too much to say—none of it clear—but I held back, not wanting to fill up the night with my words. As I was silent, I sensed that the night and the wind were enough, more than enough.

"At least," I whispered lamely, "the night is beautiful."

I don't remember what else we said. He walked, I followed, we stopped; I tried to touch him. He backed away, but not too far. We were still together, our shadows linked. "Change isn't bad," I said, but it felt like throwing pennies into a lake.

We came to our white picket fence. Then as we opened the gate, he turned to me:

"It's just that—" he began.

"What?"

"Sometimes I—"

"Sometimes you what?"

Then the dam broke, and his feelings began tumbling out: "I worry you're going to die, I worry when I come home you'll be dead"; "I worry nothing will be the same"; "I feel like I'm going to lose everything." Even the flowers, as we passed, seemed quiet, quiet but alert, the heavy hydrangeas especially, weighted to the ground, listening.

What should I say? What did one say? But at the same time I still had too much to say. "This is how people feel at your age"; "You're not where you were, and you're not where you will be"; "I felt that way too." I remembered my own sorrow at twelve, how I felt homesick, even when I was home—especially when I was home. The first feeling of the present not feeling altogether real: as if it were being viewed from a distance. A refocusing of a lens. I wanted to tell him how much I loved him, how vividly I remembered when he was two, and he was mine alone; how proud I am of him, and how much I know he will be all right in the world. We talked. Maybe I said one or two things.

Once in our house, I was suddenly exhausted. I had had enough. In the kitchen, the hall, back in the kitchen—he was following me from room to room, gesturing with his open hands, speaking from his heart.

"Everything is going away," he was saying.

I turned to him. "OK, let's stop for now," I said. "Let me make you some tea."

But he was not ready to stop; he was just getting warmed up. He continued following me as I pulled the tea off the shelf—peppermint—and focused on the box. He was speaking of how terrified he was of death. While I dunked the tea bag, I thought, "There is a way I cannot touch him, this life of his."

I handed him the tea. I went into the bathroom and closed the door. I stepped into the shower. But he was knocking on the door. I cracked open the curtain from the steaming shower and stuck my head out and yelled, "What?"

And he called, "Please, I just want to say one more thing."

"What?"

"I only know two things for sure in my life," I heard beyond the steam. "I only know the present and that one day I'll die. Those are the only things I know for certain."

"Let's talk when I get out," I said, and shoved the curtain back in place. But he knocked again, in that polite urgent way he has.

"What?"

"But what will come between?" he pleaded. "What will my life be like?"

Again I ducked back in, and yanked the curtain closed, as if I were fed up, enough is enough, but really I was feeling stunned by the intensity of the commencement of his adolescence. Shutting the curtain was like setting a painting on a black background, which only serves to highlight all that is within. Standing amid that steam, and water, I closed myself in there.

But he continued knocking, and then banging on the bathroom door, and really desperate for it to stop this time, I shouted through the steam, "Enough! Nobody's going to die this minute!" and he got mad, and threw open the door, flicked the bathroom light off, and I was standing in the shower in the dark, which was actually a relief. I leaned my head against the wall and knew that his questions couldn't be answered, not by me. Nor could they be improved upon.

❧ ❧ ❧

The moon is bright. The sky is violet. Dan has come home from work, tall, an exciting aura of the city around him. He is carrying the newspaper. He kisses me hello, his skin warm, and goes inside. I am still sitting in the yard, my body stirring. I am thinking of how brave one has to be to set out alone. I watch the fireflies. The lights of the houses have come on.

I get up, creakily. The grass is cold. The two books I've read today are lying facedown, in exactly the way we were told never to leave them, since this could break their spines. But I leave them. They have turned their backs on me, and their faces are muffled in the earth. I walk to the gate, which is still faintly glowing.

"I can't go with you," I imagine calling after Alex when he descends the path. "But here—take a book." (Which book?)

"Take a book," says the French philosopher Georges Poulet. "You will find it offering, opening itself. It is this openness of the book which I find so moving. A book is not shut in by its contours, is not walled up as in a fortress. It asks nothing better than to exist outside itself, or to let you exist in it."

* * *

"Ma," Alex calls out from the door. "When are you coming in?"

"Soon," I call.

"What are we having for dinner?"

"Pizza," I say. Then I add, "Come out."

"Why?"

"It's so beautiful—"

"I'm too cold. I want to stay in."

But he comes toward me, his shadow enormous, black, filling the lawn. As he gets closer, the smell of chlorine intensifies. He is as tall as my shoulder.

"Was it fun in the pool?"

"I guess. School's not for a while is it?"

I don't reply. We both know the answer.

"I'm worried about school," he whispers.

I touch his arm. "What about?"

His voice gets louder: "And I don't want my piano lessons to start again!"

"Let's not talk about it right now," I say. We've been talking about this on and off all summer. "We'll see."

"No, not 'We'll see.' I hate him. I'm not sitting with him that whole time anymore. It's been five years. It's enough. I hate piano. Not piano, just him. It's my life!"

"OK, OK, I understand." I make up my mind. "I'll look for someone else. I'll try to find someone you'll like more. Would that make you feel better?"

He moves closer to me. We stand together.

"It was fun today," he says quietly.

"It looked fun."

He drops his voice confidingly. "You know that older kid who was there? He's going into eighth. He said he likes *Blazing Saddles.*" He has dropped his voice to a whisper. "He said Mel Brooks is the funniest."

"That's so great," I say. We are partaking of some complex coded dialogue now, one we've had hundreds of times, whenever we discuss matters relating to comedy, especially Mel. There is something going on underneath our conversation I don't understand, but happiness floods through us. It is as if Mel is ours, our relative that we've just found out someone knows and adores. When Mel is loved, we feel fuller, taller.

I click the gate securely shut. We go in for the night.

Chapter Three

A sudden cold snap extinguishes the bright roses along the fence. Summer is over just like that, and the yard looks littered and strange. My children return to school, and I stand in the doorway.

My job—I run a creative arts program for children, called Story Shop—doesn't begin until late October. When it does, I will be buckled into an exacting routine, but for now, for this brief period, I am free. I clean up the rushed breakfast dishes. I do a load of wash. My street is empty, and when I step out again, into the fading grass, it is cheerful. Full sunshine lights the yard again; not all the roses are dead, and the black-eyed Susans are ablaze. I rake. The rake makes a satisfying sound through the leaves. As I rake, more leaves drift down.

At midmorning I drive to the library in the next town, as I have been doing lately. I like to go there, because, unlike in my own library, I rarely see anyone I know, and I like the anonymity. The library stands high on a hill, and my body hums from the climb. Inside, the leather seats are pleasantly shabby, and it is quiet.

The children's librarian, who is stamping books at the front desk, is a sturdy woman, with a serene face and tidy, pale hair. She presses the ink down definitively, and the whiteness of her nails when she presses suggests to me a certain bottled-up aggression. "Good morning," I say. I know she hears me, but she does not look up.

There is some tension between us, although it could all be in my imagination. It seemed to start last week. We had been alone; she was shelving books. "Excuse me," I said pleasantly (I thought), "but when we were kids, didn't we used to read books that were less . . . catastrophic?"

I wasn't expecting great collegiality, just a small exchange. She had always seemed cordial enough. I certainly didn't expect her to be as tense as she was at that moment; she angled away from me slightly, and didn't miss a beat in her shelving. Had I insulted her somehow?

Suddenly I sensed that I had wandered into controversial territory, and that my questioning could be perceived as provocative. I recalled Alex's compassionate language arts teacher extolling the beauty of the books, how they made children cry, as if this were the pinnacle of something to be desired. These grim books were *in*. These books were nothing if not sensitive, and my critique of them rendered me, well, insensitive. A bully. Cold. Was that it? Outrage flared up in me. What made these books—an image of miserable faces came to mind—synonymous with progress?

"Don't you think there's an excessive amount of angst here?" I persisted. And then when I saw her mouth tighten and the telltale whitening fingertips strangle the book cart, I asked softly, "Weren't our books cozier?"

When she spoke, it was with a slight Texas accent I hadn't noticed before. "Oh, these realistic sad books are very popular," she said mildly. "Teachers love them. They win all the awards."

"So?" I snapped. Then I said something that immediately I regretted, since it sounded like I was calling out the title of a Country and Western song: "Are they worthy of love?" I cried.

She shrugged her shoulders and turned away. Later, after I embarrassedly made my way over to a table, having begun tentatively to pluck books with glaring teens on their covers, she walked over to me—she was wearing ballet shoes, I noticed—and handed me a hefty book. "This might help you," she said. I thanked her, and took it, but the insinuation that I needed help made me uncomfortable.

It was a reference book called *Children's Literature in the Elementary School,* into which she had stuck a yellow sticky note where, presumably, she thought I should read:

"Realistic fiction helps children enlarge their frames of reference while seeing the world from another perspective," the highlighted passage read. "Stories . . . help young people develop compassion for an understanding of human actions. . . . For many years, death was a taboo subject in children's literature. Yet, as children face the honest realities of life in books, they are developing a kind of courage for facing problems in their own lives."

Sound enough, as far as it went. I read further. But after a while, I began to wonder different things. What did it take for a young reader to draw courage from a book? I knew it was possible, of course. Even though I was very unsettled by reading *The Hundred Dresses,* by Eleanor Estes, when I was nine—a story about schoolgirls' insensitivity to a poor classmate, and the failure of any of them to stand up for the girl—I recognize that it helped me to begin to formulate some ideas about how I wanted to act, and not act. In particular, I think the book offered me the first outline of the idea that it was possible to resist the velocity of group pressure.

But more often in my reading experience, it seems, I had drawn inspiration not so much from a character's actions, or the plot, as from some moment in the language of the story, when it was revealed to me that the author was seeing the world in the same way I did. At such times, I felt pulled out from some shadow I hadn't known I'd been hiding in. I remember feeling startled, embarrassed, but strangely heartened too, for example, when I came across Alfred Kazin's book *A Walker in the City* when I was twelve: it was as if Alfred Kazin were writing specifically about me, and the secret feeling I had that my neighborhood in the upper tip of Manhattan was odd, too far from the rest of the world. "When I was a child," he wrote, "I thought we lived at the end of the world. It was the eternity of the subway ride into the city that first gave me this idea. Even the I.R.T. got tired by the time it came to us, and ran up into the open for a breath of air." The subway had always been a being to me also, in need of that fresh gulp of air, but I never guessed that another person thought this way too.

These experiences of startling recognition usually happened in a moment that I would have missed if I had been reading too fast, and when I came to such a moment, I would stop and go back over the words, even if it was just three words, or just one word, and feel so strange, and happy, as if I'd found something I had been looking for but hadn't been aware of until just that moment.

I thought about that, and other things too: What did I feel about fiction being conceived of as primarily a teaching tool? As a tool to further the notions of, say, multiculturalism, an approach that could be deliciously rich, but which seemed never able to move freely, since the strict, humorless watchdog of Political Correctness was always nipping at its heels. How had trauma—endless stories about childhood trauma—managed to garner the cachet of multiculturalism, and hence the protection of Political Correctness?

I was deep in thought, and when I looked up, I was surprised to see the librarian watching me, with a shrewdness I had not noticed in her before; she was regarding me from behind some slats in a shelf. She seemed to be trying to assess if I was learning more tolerance. I slammed the book shut with a bang.

My table at the library is by the window, a round table with a quiet luster, on which all the books I've been reading for two weeks make a precarious stack. I put my bag lunch down, and I separate the books into smaller stacks so they won't topple over.

These are books whose titles I came across on school reading lists, some that were prize winners, some recommended to me by friends and kids I know. But some books I found just by generally poking around the shelves—the children's shelves and the adjacent Young Adult section. I selected books that strove to be realistic, rather than books of fantasy, or humor, or historical fiction, because the realistic books seemed distinct from books I grew up with, whereas the other types were more familiar. I tried to choose books that promised "profound struggle."

And I have come to regard my stacks in the words of a ten-year-old girl I know: "They give me a headache in my stomach." Literary critics refer to some of the books I've assembled as "problem novels"—and *boy* do problems abound.

While making my way through them, I have encountered: kids whose parents are drunk and cruelly neglectful *(The Pigman)*, a child's uncle so demented by grief that he hallucinates his dead wife throughout the whole book *(Chasing Redbird)*, atrocities of foster care and abandonment by one's mother *(They Cage the Animals at Night; Monkey Island)*, more abandonment *(Dicey's Song; Bud, Not Buddy)*, alcoholism *(The Late, Great Me)*, kidnapping *(Ransom; The Face on the Milk Carton)*, child abuse *(Bruises; Don't Hurt Laurie)*, family violence *(Breathing Lessons)*, sexual abuse *(Speak)*, incest *(Abby, My Love)*, teen suicide *(Tunnel Vision)*, running away and child prostitution *(Steffie Can't Come Out to Play)*, teen pregnancy *(A House for Jonnie O)*, and self-mutilation *(Cut; Crosses)* —to name but a very few. Some of the books are well written and affecting. Some—many—are downright depressing, so that even if the writing is vibrant, the story told is unpleasant, weighty. Others are so sensationalistic as to read like dopey soap operas, pure and simple. *The Face on the Milk Carton*—about a teenage girl who suddenly realizes one day at breakfast that the face she sees of a missing child on the milk carton is actually her own when she was a toddler, and that in fact the adults she lives with, whom she has believed are her mother and father, must really be people who kidnapped her from her real parents years before—well—fits the last category.

While plowing through these stacks, I read around in some other texts as well, in an effort to get a handle on the nature of these novels.

"Stated broadly, and ignoring variations that inevitably exist in so large a literature," writes historian Anne Scott Macleod, "the path of American adolescent novels has been from outward to inward; from concern with the young adult's relationship to the larger community to a nearly exclusive emphasis on the adolescent's inner feelings."

Problem novels and the like sprang into existence during and after the 1960s (I probably stopped dipping into children's literature just at the moment they began). The general speculation seems to be that *The Catcher in the Rye*, by J. D. Salinger, while not intended for teenagers, was perhaps a prototype for the first problem novels, in that the story is told in the voice of a disaffected adolescent, at odds with a disappointing adult world. *Harriet the Spy*, written by Louise Fitzhugh in 1964, is also seen as an important first book in this new realm. "When in *Harriet,*" writes Anne Macleod, "an adult told a child, 'You must lie' she was doing at least two things unprecedented in mainstream children's literature: First, she was repudiating a long-observed adult responsibility to be a role model and a keeper of the moral universe for children. And second, she was letting a child, an unambiguous, preadolescent, eleven-year-old child, in on one of the untidy realities of the adult world, with no moral judgment attached." While Macleod sees *Harriet* as "symptomatic and not causative," she goes on to say, "after Fitzhugh came the Deluge."

These sensibilities set the tone for future books in this genre. Sheila Egoff, a Canadian specialist in children's literature, writes that the realistic adolescent novel, "[takes] the approach that maturity can be attained only through a severe testing of soul and self, [featuring] some kind of shocking 'rite of passage' such as the uprooting of a child's life by war, the death of a close friend . . ." She defines the problem novel as a subgenre of the realistic adolescent novel: it tends to be narrower in focus, less rich in narrative scope, and at times feels "as if the writers had begun with the problem rather than the plot or characters." The problem novel is most often about a "child defined by the terminology of pain." Egoff further delineates some of its characteristics:

- The protagonist is alienated and hostile toward adults.
- Some relief from unhappiness comes from a relationship with an adult outside the family.
- The story is often told in the first person, and is often confessional and self-centered.
- The narrative is told from the point of view of an ordinary child, often in the vernacular; vocabulary is limited; tone is often flat, and emotionally detached.

- Dialogue predominates.
- The settings are urban, usually in New York or California.
- Sexuality is openly and frequently discussed.
- Parents are absent, either physically or emotionally.

I have found these observations applicable to many of the books I've read, although in the more recently published books, death, rather than sex, seems the primary theme, and locations are not limited to the coastal cities. And while many are written primarily in dialogue, often in the vernacular, there appears to be a growing body of realistic, problem-driven books written in a densely elegiac language, borrowing, perhaps, from the mood of the adult memoir.

A desolate feeling in many of the novels prevails. In virtually all the books I've read, the character's mother is dead, missing, or nonfunctional.

The ethos of many of these books, if there is one, seems not to be "Love Makes the World Go Round," or "Only Connect," or "There's No Place Like Home," or even primarily "Be Brave." Instead, "Only Survive" or "At Least You Have Yourself (since you can't rely on anyone else)" is more to the point. Also: "What You See Is All There Is." Also: "Lower Your Expectations (the most you can expect from life is small kindnesses from strangers and the fact that you can get up in the morning and go on)."

The narrative voices in these novels, whether the story is told in first person or third, seem to share a particular quality. Lack of humor, the tackling of traumatic themes, and a relentless earnestness all come to mind, as well as their often confessional tone. But another aspect also links this group.

While the books are most often told in the voice of a child narrator, or narrator identified with a child, and, in some, the child's language might sound more or less believable, many of the books rarely deliver what I consider an authentic child's perspective. Something feels false. Something essential feels missing.

What is it? The answer is this: No child I have known experiences "reality" only in terms of what happens—"the facts." For all children, except in cases of extreme pathology, there is to a greater or lesser degree a corresponding magical, imaginative counterpart to experience. This dimension does not have to be fully conscious, but exists nevertheless. By "magic" I do not mean (only) manifest magic, as in the child's belief or wish that he could turn invisible or fly. In fact, as children get older, such manifest magic is understood increasingly to be the exclusive province of dramatic play and art, distinct from reality. But latent magic continues to abound in the everyday. There is chatter among trees. The world vibrates with connections, and within these connections the world is more dangerous (than for adults), since shadows can be alive, and menacing, but the world is more providential also, since allies can be found in rocks, in the hopeful sunlight, and the like. Within this universe, the child is the nexus, but while he might be hindered or aided by the natural world, he is never alone. The point is that in childhood, and well into early adolescence (and in all poetic worlds), the universe is animate, or at least potentially animate, with an unseen presence.

And it is precisely this dimension to childhood experience that is absent from many realistic novels and virtually all problem novels. No magic, manifest or latent, vibrates within them. Instead, in all of these self-proclaimed realistic stories, "reality" is understood as the opposite of imagination and fantasy, as if childhood were a dream from which children must be awakened—when, in fact, reality is not divisible from imagining, for children. But in these books children's imagination is regarded as something that must be tamed, monitored, barred. The child protagonist, while presented with the darkest and most upsetting situations imaginable, is denied what in real childhood would exist in abundance: recourse to fantasy.

In problem novels, the worse the reality is, the weaker the character's imagination, and the more he must learn to just cope, by relying on himself. In reality, I think the reverse is more often true: the harsher and more stressful life is for a child, the more fecund the imagination, as if the imagination is the natural antidote, sanctuary, resting place, insulation, place for renewal. In fact, deprivation and struggle can be the inspiration to create a fictional world. I know that in my own childhood, the more alone or upset I felt, the more the universe "spoke" to me.

The book *Monkey Island,* by Paula Fox, comes to mind in this context. It is a much-lauded novel, awarded Best Book for Young Adults by the ALA and assigned as required reading in the fifth grade of a nearby school. The book details the attempt at survival by an abandoned boy, who goes to live with some homeless men in a box in the park:

> Sometimes the two men paid little attention to him, although he knew they had really taken him into their lives in the park.
>
> But on some days, there had been moments, hours, when they barely spoke to him as they went about their housekeeping, or just sat silently with grim, faraway expressions on their faces. Then he knew that his being a child, a thing he'd never thought about much before, made no difference at all. He was alone as they were alone. He was just another person, ageless, in trouble, out of ordinary life, out of the time that ruled the lives of people hurrying past the park on their way to work or home.

Fine atmospheric writing. Meritorious for its telling of a terrible cultural problem. But it is only accurate, it seems to me, in describing a child's life from the outside, as it were, but not accurate in rendering how a child might actually be experiencing that life. If a child lives in a box, because his mother deserted him, wouldn't there be things he'd be thinking, daydreams, theories he'd be spinning, flights of fantasy, terrifying and otherwise, unique to him, to try to concoct meaning, and garner some inner bounty? Some imaginative remaking of the whole situation? (To say nothing of the fact that such revelations about the child's creative emotional coping mechanisms would make the story that much more bearable, and more meaningful to the young reader.)

But *Monkey Island* is faithful only to the small facts that make up the boy's sad days; the book stays close to the ground. What he eats, what he wears. In the end the book is not so much about an actual person as about a terrible situation.

It is as if Paula Fox doesn't regard the boy fully as a child, at least not enough to give him a child's consciousness. Even if the facts of his existence are similar to those of an adult, does that mean he experiences them the same way an adult would? I think not.

Children also do not play in problem novels. Or if they do, the play sequences are never woven seamlessly into life, the way, for example, Huck in *Huckleberry Finn* describes his playing life. (Huck, even though he has a whole array of family troubles, like children in problem novels, is the very antithesis of the problem novel character.) Huck's narrative moves in and out of descriptions of play and fantasy episodes. When he pretends to plot crimes with Tom Sawyer and a gang of other boys, deep in damp caves in the middle of the night, pages are devoted to descriptions of the oath pledged among the boys, involving exchanges of blood and promises of murder if the secret of their gang is revealed by any. Huck describes the end of one such night:

> Little Tommy Barnes was asleep now, and when they waked him up he was scared, and cried, and said he wanted to go home to his ma, and didn't want to be a robber any more.
>
> So they all made fun of him, and called him crybaby, and that made him mad, and he said he would go straight and tell all the secrets. But Tom give him five cents to keep quiet, and said we would all go home and meet next week, and rob somebody and kill some people.

In other words, the story told through Huck's eyes portrays play the way it really feels to children: deliciously real, but at the same time, *not exactly the same* as reality. Play and fantasy are facets of the prism through which life is experienced.

Many of the novels I've read seem not to regard play in this way. Any play sequences are described in a highly self-conscious, guarded way, and are put in the story to teach a lesson. The "secret world" in *Bridge to Terabithia* is a perfect example of how fantasy is regarded in these books. The very bridge in question causes the death of a child. (Fantasy is dangerous.) And Jess's realization at the end of the book—indeed the book's epiphany, as it were—is that to grow up he must give up imaginative wanderings in favor of "reality."

Huck's river, seen through the lens of his imagination, "speaks" to him, but in a problem novel, nature never speaks or offers consolation. That is because, as I've suggested, no unseen presence exists. It is as if a child calls out, but there is no echo. When Huck looks out into the world, the world he sees is animate, sentient, responsive:

> When it was dark I set by my camp fire smoking, and feeling pretty well satisfied; but by and by it got sort of lonesome, and so I went and set on the bank and listened to the current swashing along, and counted the stars and drift logs and rafts that come down, and then went to bed; there ain't no better way to put in time when you are lonesome; you can't stay so, you soon get over it.

But when a child in a problem novel looks into nature, bereft of imaginative powers, the world never is particularized in any way, is never a character like Huck's river. Instead, that child sees only himself.

> I snuck off [says the thirteen-year-old narrator in *Chasing Redbird*], raced up the hill behind the barn and down the other side, and ran along the creek until I came to the start of my trail. I felt like I owned the trail because I discovered it.... I cleared away grass and debris, uncovering a row of similar stones, leading in a line from the creek on up the hill. Zinnia Taylor: explorer!

The woods are barely noticed, full as they are of "debris" and "similar stones," and instead exist only as an expression or reflection of the narrator, or simply as a barrier to get through, or a way for Zinnia to define herself in relation to them: explorer. The world qua world—larger, unknown, suggesting revelation that springs from other than oneself, as a mediating force through which one can be transformed—does not exist.

But while the children in problem novels don't have rich imaginations, they are given mood states: they are depressed, nervous, worried. And they often feel very guilty. One child I know remarked, "In those books the kids always hate themselves." Many characters are portrayed as feeling that they are the cause of the terrible things that occur.

This feeling of being the center of the universe—the cause of everything—is authentic enough to childhood, but where this omnipotence reigns in child thinking, doesn't a whole world of other fantasies—comforting, deep ones—exist alongside it? Why deprive the child narrators of the rest of their experience?

Maybe because these narrators aren't really children.

Sometimes I have suspected this is the case. In *Chasing Redbird,* the story begins with the narrator interpreting a sampler on the wall of her aunt's kitchen: "*Life is a bowl of spaghetti . . . every now and then you get a meatball . . .* My name is Zinny (for Zinnia) Taylor. I live with a slew of brothers and sisters . . . You feel like everybody's spaghetti is all tangled in one pot. . . . My mother was having babies right and left."

Maybe this sounds close enough to how a thirteen-year-old might talk, but in fact, something feels off. It does not represent how any thirteen-year-old I know is experiencing life: from a distance.

Here's what I mean. An adult telling a story about when he was a child (for example in memoir) has a lot of latitude in rendering childhood experience; he can articulate some aspects of experience that might not have been available for articulation back then, but, given the grandeur of hindsight, can now be pushed through into words. This isn't so with child narrators who claim to be children here and now: we must believe that they are children speaking. To report on the state of one's family at thirteen, by summing up as Zinny does, strikes me as more in the vein of observations by an adult made, say, after psychotherapy, when after slogging through all the stories and particulars, one has earned a sudden vista from which to look back, in a reflective, slightly detached way, and sum up: "Man, there were a slew of kids in that house!" In fact, summing up itself draws from an older sensibility, because it means you've come to the end of something, or at least a breathing spot, and can reflect. To encounter a thirteen-year-old character who is so alone as to refer to all her brothers and sisters as a "slew" of them suggests to me a character who is either just plain inauthentic, precocious in the extreme, or disassociated from the flow of the present.

To speak of one's mother as "having babies right and left" may not seem to warrant critique; the phrasing is unremarkable enough. But in conjunction with the rest of the language, and the rest of the character, this phrasing further suggests a weird point of view for a child to have about her mother, as if this child has access to a detached view of her mother, from which she can assess her utterly apart from herself, and effectively sum her up. Such a detached perception, when it finally does come in real life, is felt as a crisis and signals that a leap has been made into adolescence proper—a far cry from the experience of a child, or even an early adolescent. This narrative voice is a bit too knowing to feel authentic to me: it feels more like the voice of someone looking back: an adult disguised as a child.

From my paper bag, I pull out my illicit cup of coffee and hide it behind the stack of books. The only person near me is a quiet man, quite elderly, wearing a bright, madras shirt. He is reading a newspaper, spread open on his table. He is holding himself very still, both thick hands lying open-palmed, as if he is showing me he has nothing to hide. He is the only one near, but I sense that I should shove the coffee even farther behind my stack, since no food is allowed here. I pull out a hard-boiled egg and a little packet of salt, and I begin to crack the shell, which comes off in a satisfying, smooth swipe. He doesn't look up. I take a bite, but worry that the smell is too strong, and put it back in its tin foil. I also have brought a bar of halvah, which seems safer to eat, and I nick off a corner and suck.

Next to me is a huge window, obscured by thin blue blinds. Through the blinds, I regard the river, while I am eating and sipping. I am surprised to see the river moving at a faster clip than the bright, carefree morning suggested. It is as if there is an urgency to the river, as if the cold weather is closer at hand than I thought.

I open another book in my stack—*American Children's Literature and the Construction of Childhood,* by Gail Schmunk Murray. It is a nice size book, small, not too thick, with a peaceful golden cover. It is part of a series called Twayne's History of American Childhood. It was published in 1998. I turn it over in my hands before I open it. It promises to contextualize, as the historians say, the advent of the problem novel. Why and when did the problem novel come into being?

In her introduction, Murray argues that "the meaning of childhood is socially constructed and . . . its meaning has changed over time."

> Of course, society has never spoken with one voice, but in every era, except perhaps the present one, a dominant culture has prevailed. Books written for children reveal this dominant culture, reflect its behavioral standards . . . On the whole, children's literature is a conservative medium. Clergy, teachers, parents, and writers have all used it to shape morals, control information, model proper behavior, delineate gender roles,

> and reinforce class, race, and ethnic separation. Historically, children's fiction has not encouraged creativity, exploration of behaviors, or self-expression.

"Children's books," Murray observes, "often tell us much more about the image of the ideal child that society would like to produce than they do about real children."

What is the ideal child like now? I wonder.

"Independent," I answer myself instantly. I picture a child, boy or girl, trooping alone through a hot, New York City street. The child is shouldering an enormous backpack, uncomplaining. "A real trooper."

And what was the ideal child like when I was young, nearly forty years ago? I know this instantly too: The ideal girl—at least the ideal that spoke loudest to me—was pure and good, charitable, almost selfless. I am thinking of *Pollyanna* and *Anne of Green Gables,* books written in the early part of the twentieth century, but which did not feel outdated when I was young. An ideal boy was more like Tom Sawyer or Huck Finn: fundamentally kind and just, but adventurous, even wayward. A risk taker. But trooping, with its suggestion of grim soldierly determination, didn't figure in when I was young. How did the good girl, or the wayward adventurer boy, morph into "trooper"?

I flip to the chapter called "Idealized Realism, 1920–1950," which, even though I was born in 1956, seems to sum up in its title something about the books I grew up on. "It is hard to find a more turbulent era in American history," Murray writes, "than the three decades bracketed in this chapter." But children's literature of this period, she notes, did not reflect any of the country's upheaval; instead, books offered an optimistic world-view:

> Childhood and particularly the nuclear family that nurtured children was idealized and modeled with unceasing repetition in children's books. It was almost as if authors consciously sought to remove any unpleasantness of real life—whether discrimination against minorities, suffering and death, the consumerism of the twenties, or the effects of the Great Depression.

And then more:

> In the face of an increasingly pluralistic culture, authors of children's books emphasized nostalgia and distant culture, middle class themes. . . . New authors sought to create more realistic settings, whether in the past or in a specific American region, such as a Wyoming ranch or a Florida swamp. They strove for exacting physical detail and attempted to realistically portray children's abilities and emotions. Yet the family setting into which this more realistic child was placed remained highly idealized.

I am reminded here of a succinct sentence written by Anne Macleod, summing up the same period: "On the whole, the outer world as pictured in children's fiction was benign, an extension of home kindness toward children."

All this rings true. Weren't all our books then safe, with the presence of someone, some kind adult, however crusty or obscure, watching over us? Wasn't there someone who, when we felt most alone, turned out to have been there all along?

I don't remember feeling anxiety upon opening a book.

Somebody was in charge in those books. And if it wasn't

a character, an adult or a wise animal, maybe I'm just remembering my feeling about the narrative voice itself back then: omniscient, disembodied (never a first-person child narrator). Maybe because it spoke over and above, this narrative voice had a kind of sweeping grandeur for me, echoing my feelings about an overseeing God, or nature, or a protective, all-knowing adult.

And those narrators would never tell us stories that left us desolate. Even the youngest readers knew this. We knew from the outset who would never die: main characters, children, parents. Or if someone central was killed off, if tragedy struck, death would be cocooned in a kind of enviable angelic aura (e.g., Little Eva in *Uncle Tom's Cabin*). Or death was otherwise neatly subsumed into the story, and over before you knew it, making it seem remarkably manageable.

I remember reading a novel about the Holocaust when I was twelve, called *The Silver Sword*, by Ian Serraillier, about children whose parents are taken away by Nazis, and who then had to fend for themselves in the woods and abandoned basements. But even though the story was tense and felt profoundly real, and I knew about the Holocaust from my parents and grandparents, I loved that book. I don't recall feeling overwhelmed or bleak, the way, say, Alex seems to feel about some of the books he is asked to read. It didn't give me nightmares. In fact, didn't I used to play that I was somehow also an orphan, hiding from the Nazis, just like in the book? How had that story been handled such that it left me feeling exhilarated, rather than hopeless?

I remember that the children had verve. They formed a kind of ragtag gang of orphans; they had a certain jaunty cheer. They were inventive. And even though the world they moved through was terribly dangerous, the mere fact that they were children gave them a special status, an aura of protection.

Later I find the book on the library shelves, one old tattered copy, published in 1959. I come upon a section that I seem to have remembered all these years: the children, who have been hiding in a barn, and are exhausted, and scared, are discovered by a farmer, who might or might not turn them over to the authorities. He orders the children to his farmhouse. But a certain fairy tale atmosphere prevails:

> There were gay window-boxes on the sills of the farmhouse, gay with flowers. On the scrubbed table in the kitchen a breakfast of coffee and rolls had been laid.
>
> "Emma," called the farmer. "Four visitors for breakfast—four tattered bundles of mischief from Poland."
>
> A plump and comfortable-looking lady shook hands with each of them in turn and, welcoming them to the table, went to fetch more breakfast.

The children are refreshed. The scene is radiant. It is as if the story dips itself periodically into a clear lake that washes away the grime of life, leaving the children's spirits renewed. While the tone here is like a fairy tale's, it also captures something realistic about childhood for me: Alex and Clair, and most children I know, seem to have access to this clear lake, this radiance and capacity for renewal.

While I am thinking about this, the old man sitting near me turns a page of his newspaper, rattling and shaking the paper to get the kinks out. He will not read even one word until the whole paper complies. I watch him coaxing the page flat with his thick hand. Finally, it lies smooth on the table. He shifts in his seat, and lets out a little grunt of contentment. His eyebrows, which are unwieldy, are arched in interest. He begins reading intently. His slow, serious reading, his feet planted squarely on the floor, his periodic grunting, are engrossing to watch. Beyond him, the sky has grown cloudy. The coming rain casts a restful light between us.

I think of my father as I watch him: my father from long ago, when I was five, and he told me important things about the world. I remember his very rich, serious voice, which had the tone of burnished wood, his direct brown eyes, the feeling of his fingers holding my hands. "There was a man named Adolf Hitler," he told me. "He was a very bad man." I remember staring back into his eyes, not daring to move, so huge was this confidence. But from the energy of his voice, I knew that the danger he was about to describe was something that had already passed; goodness had triumphed. "Hitler thought the world would be better if there were only people in it who looked the same," my father told me. I noted the way his lips looked a little white while he spoke, which revealed a bewildering rage I had never seen in him before. "Hitler wanted everyone to be blonde, and have blue eyes. He tried to kill all the Jews."

I think of my father as I watch the man pick up his newspaper and open it, giving an aggressive whip of his wrist when the paper droops even slightly. His face is hidden behind the paper. This too relays my father: as if all worldly concerns were contained in print, as if in the act of reading he was surveying the landscape—the lay of the land—to make sure we were safe.

I rest my head on my folded arms, and angle my face into the weak sunlight. The change of light conjures the eeriness of elementary school while a storm was brewing. It was briefly intimate, the way everyone was drawn together. But it was so formal, even then. I missed my parents when I was in school. I wanted to go home.

I am staring at my egg, so perfectly stout, even with one nibble out of its side. I am remembering Dick and Jane readers, the very first schoolbooks. The drawings of chubby little Jane from so long ago, with her blonde curls and her gossamer pinafore, and Dick, in shorts, the very picture of a "lad."

I can remember the details of the illustrations so clearly, perfectly, as if I had seen them just a minute ago. I can see their yard, dappled with green light, encircled by a white fence. The translucency of the ink.

And I remember how it felt to open the readers each morning. Like I was peering right into their yard, like I was a huge child who had crept up, who was watching smaller, strange children in their yard, without them knowing. I remember distinctly the sense that they were vaguely real, that if they became aware of me, if they for some reason looked up, it would not be altogether a good thing.

The parents were called Mother and Father, which I found shocking, that children might refer to their parents so formally. And Mother and Father came out into the green yard once in a while, on special occasions. They were young, laughing, trim. Mother had such a small waist, and wore a little belt around her dress.

But even when Mother and Father weren't in the pictures, their shadows seemed to fall across the lawn, as if they were standing just out of the frame, always present. If there wasn't this proximity, how else could Dick and Jane be so carefree? Which was how they seemed: wagons and balls scattered casually on the lawn (in my New York City life, I had never seen a real wagon); the dog yipping around without a leash. The parents oversaw everything. The white picket fence encircled the children. The continual joy of the parents impressed me: it seemed incited by nothing in particular, except by the same joy the children felt about their ball, their dog, life in general.

This was the feeling in all our books then, wasn't it? This sense of special enclosure, the presence of adults. I remember that the boundaries of the illustrations did not quite fit into the edge of the pages, were not exactly neat and trim, but left fluttery by the paint brush, as if this neighborhood was truly airborne, blown in from a corner of the world full of fresh breezes, where it was always summer.

I continue to lie on my arms. Against the darkening sky, I can see my own eyes looking back at me in the glass, watching myself, remembering the pictures, and myself as a girl reader.

What if Dick and Jane had looked up, beyond the page, and seen me—the huge face of a dark girl?

How did Jewish enter into this? What made me know—although I never then could have formed it into words—that Dick and Jane and Mother and Father weren't Jews?

That they had never heard of Jews, that they might not like Jews? What mood would cross their faces if they realized who had been watching them all this time?

No Jew lived in that book.

I sit up. This is what I remember from those first books. The children in them were safe, and enclosed. It was sunny there. But sometimes I felt left out.

Chapter Four

"[A] new construction of childhood emerged during the 1960's," Gail Murray argues in her chapter "Child Liberation 1950–1990":

> It recognized that children could not always be protected from the dangers and sorrows of real life; they might be better prepared to cope with pain if adults did not try to protect them from it.... The boundaries that had protected children and adolescents from adult responsibilities throughout the nineteenth century and the first half of the twentieth century became much more permeable.... Such previously defined adult issues as sexuality and suffering entered the realm of childhood.

Or, as Anne Macleod sums up: "By the middle of the 1960's, political and social changes leaned hard on the crystal cage that had surrounded children's literature for decades. It cracked, and the world flowed in."

I view the stacks of books on my table. *The Pigman,* by Paul Zindel, written in 1968, is a book I find especially haunting, one that most seems to sum up this new "construction of childhood." It never fell into my hands when I was young, but a neighbor's daughter read it in sixth grade. She hated it, said it was "weird" and "depressing."

It is weird and depressing. But it's intriguing too. It stands out from the rest of the problem novels, maybe because—unlike in *Bridge to Terabithia,* say—no adult viewpoint comes in to wrap the story up, bring it down to earth, pay lip service to its "meaning." *The Pigman*, in a sense, is unchaperoned by any sobering adult sensibility, is told straight in the alternating voices of two teenagers, and ends disastrously. It does not serve as a moral tale; the reader does not sense any hidden agenda, or at least not a familiar one, on the part of the writer.

The two teenagers, John and Lorraine, come from unhappy families—neglectful, unaffectionate, cold, bitter. Such a portrayal of family life would have been unthinkable in books published less than a decade earlier.

John describes his family at the dinner table:

> "Your father sold over three hundred lots today," the Old Lady said, like she was patting a cocker spaniel on the head. Bore has a seat on the Coffee Exchange, and if he sells more than two hundred lots in a day, he's in a good mood. Anything less than that and there's trouble.
>
> "It's like pulling teeth," Bore returned, slightly embarrassed but pleased with the praise. He cut deep into his steak on his plate. "Wait until you start working John."
>
> "I have to get the dessert," the Old Lady said, violently polishing a teaspoon and dashing out to the kitchen. She always gets terrified if it looks like my father and I are going to have any type of discussion.

Lorraine lives alone with her mother. Their relationship is complex and fraught, as can be glimpsed from the following scene. The mother is speaking first:

> "I came home late last night . . . and the girl down the street was in a car, necking like a slut."
>
> "Maybe she's engaged to that boy."

> "I don't care. Just don't let me catch you in a car if you know what's good for you."
>
> She always warns me about getting into cars and things like that. . . . Beware of men is what she's really saying. They have dirty minds, and they're only after one thing.
>
> But now I understand her a little. I think the only man she really hates is my father—even though he's dead.

The teenagers are predictably lonely and confused, and the ache for missing emotional warmth and security pulsates through the book. In an attempt to "[look] for a way out of their numbness of being lonely" they enter, accidentally, into the life of an elderly widower, Mr. Pignali, whom they call Pigman. He is a vulnerable little man, in need of human contact himself. The kids befriend him, sort of, and they form a makeshift "family," but at the same time they take advantage of him—most terribly by allowing their friends to trash his apartment while he's in the hospital, recovering from a heart attack. But, overall, it is accurate to say that the kids and the adult have reversed roles in this book: John and Lorraine are more functional than Pigman (he is deluded, thinking his dead wife is still alive), and they take him to the zoo, as parents would take a child. He is portrayed as utterly innocent, to the point of being gullible, and the kids get a kind of reprieve from their empty homes while they hang out in his apartment and construct a kind of childhood—using him as the child. But the tension between kindness and enormous neediness, between exploitation and moral ambiguity, is nerve-racking.

Mr. Pignali dies, in part as a result of their recklessness, because he is overcome by the sight of his ransacked apartment. Yet while the kids feel guilty and broken, they take from the experience what all kids are expected to learn in problem novels, namely: you have no one but yourself.

John relays the aftermath of Mr. Pignali's death:

> "We murdered him," [Lorraine] screamed.
>
> I wanted to yell at her, tell her he had no business fooling around with kids. I wanted to tell her he had no right going backward. When you grow up, you're not supposed to go back. Trespassing—that's what he had done.
>
> We had trespassed too—been where we didn't belong and we were being punished for it.
>
> There was no one to blame anymore. No Bores or Old Ladies. . . . And there was no place to hide.

A friend tells me she read *The Pigman* when she was a teenager, years ago, when it first came out. She said the book meant a lot to her, that she cherished it, that it told her something about boys and girls together that she hadn't read anywhere before. This remark reminds me of a critic's observation: "Individual readers come to each story at a slightly different point in their life's journey. If nobody comes between them and the book, they may discover within it some insight they require, a rest they long for, a point of view that challenges their own, a friend they may cherish for life." My friend felt that the book was "secret and private."

Would I have liked this book years ago? Would it have been the same experience to read it at twelve—as my neighbor's daughter did—as, say, at fifteen? Would it be the same to read it on one's own, in "secret and private," as to have to read it as part of a school curriculum?

I try to remember twelve again. I looked like a doll I once had, not Barbie, but a pretty, polite child doll named Betsy McCall, who had dark bangs, and who looked sweet and sporty in her underwear, her bloomers, and smooth undershirt, trimmed with a bow. I had entered puberty, but was still trying to remain on the childhood side. I tried to smile as much as I could. Actually I felt wobbly. I always wore tight knee socks, which I secretly pretended were leg braces that held me up from falling.

My family was coming apart; my parents would later divorce. I knew these things, but at twelve I didn't think about my life, at least not consciously, in terms of a sweeping narrative: "My family is coming apart; I'm miserable." I tried instead to "keep going" in some way, as I always had. I didn't have a new way of apprehending the world, so I stuck with the old. Events—fighting, crying, new surges of feelings within—were relegated to things that happened in other rooms, and that I could tiptoe past.

To read about the anarchic world of *The Pigman,* at twelve (unthinkable at eight) would have been more than I could handle. Like a direct assault. It would have been like ripping down one structure, the only structure I had, before anything else was in its place. (*A Tree Grows in Brooklyn,* on the other hand, ripped down nothing: it constructed something.)

How about at fifteen?

By then a lot had changed. I had a boyfriend; I was in open war with my parents; I had been thrown out of school. My fake smiling and tentativeness had given way to lawlessness, bravado. Every time I destroyed something, I felt free. Underneath, my terror was great—of emptiness, of disappearing, of desolation. I had the feeling of barely holding on. But still I had something I didn't have at twelve: a sense of how I was viewed by others: positively by boys, negatively by adults. I had landed, somehow, or at least had acknowledged to myself that I was on a "long strange trip."

So would I have been thrilled by the freedom of those irate and rebellious kids in *The Pigman?* Would it have given me "courage"? Would I have come upon this book that described a reality I knew to be possible, and felt, "Hey, I'm not alone"? That someone, namely the book's author Paul Zindel, saw the world as I did?

It might have been fascinating to read, if it had come at the right time.

I remember my neighbor telling me that when her daughter was twelve, and read *The Pigman* in school, the girl found it disturbing, and ate a whole box of Mallomars while reading, after which she felt sick. My neighbor mentioned that she wondered at the time if that gorging might have been, at least in part, a response to an empty feeling generated by the book. How utterly strange to be required to read such a dark, potent book about adolescent rage and depression, by one's own school. My neighbor added that the teacher who had assigned the book was not particularly sensitive. Would a more intuitive teacher have made the experience better?

Maybe part of the problem for Alex, and perhaps for my neighbor's daughter, is how so much of school reading is "packaged." "This is a timed essay test," reads one of Alex's mimeographed sheets from his English class. "You have ten minutes on each question. You will be graded for grammar, and accuracy. One: List lessons in the book that the teens learned. Explain. Two: What values are expressed in the story? Choose one, respect, trust, etc. and write about how the characters enact these values."

"We can't ever say we don't like the books," Alex has said.

"But what if you explain why you don't like them, and critique the book?" I asked.

His teacher, he said, "thinks if you're not liking the books, you're not reading them closely enough."

It seems that *The Pigman* is a bit of a revolutionary book, both because it was among the first of its kind, and because, if a teenager comes upon it at the right time, it might echo a certain feeling of being an outlaw, an outcast. It might be exciting to find that such a book exists, that art can be made from edgy, unclear feelings.

But to find such a book as part of assigned reading, accompanied with worksheets, and tests, and grades, to be asked to chart the book's symbolism and fill in right answers seems deadly. The book has become appropriated by the Board of Education, and now constitutes "Official Knowledge." You can't have it both ways: a reader feeling intimacy with the writer and the text, and the text being appropriated by someone else.

Reading a book on your own, in "secret and private" (or with an intuitive teacher), might be like coming upon a wild landscape, where you are a pioneer, a wilderness whose meaning reveals itself to you over time. Reading a book accompanied with lessons and right answers and tests and grades—especially in the world of uncharted emotion—is like coming to a landscape, maybe an intriguing one, but finding that it is owned by, say, Pepsi, and the park is a tourist site. You are told what paths you can go on and what is off-limits. Perhaps you are offered souvenirs for a small fee.

"How can the sightseer recover the Grand Canyon?" writes Walker Percy on the theme of the difficulty in seeing. "It may be recovered by leaving the beaten track. The tourist leaves the tour. . . . He sees the canyon by avoiding all the facilities for seeing the canyon."

I get up and stretch. The old man has dozed off, his newspaper folded neatly into a square. His head is thrown back on the stalk of his thin neck; his Adam's apple protrudes. He is snoring gently. I return to my seat, and through the thin blue slats of the blinds, the sky is moving swiftly. There are white caps on the water; the storm is brewing. I eat my egg.

I wanted to be a writer when I was fifteen, and as I look out through the slats, to the open, grey sky, I remember the feeling of wanting to write but having no idea what to say. I only knew that I didn't want to write about "troubles at home." What I wanted to express was inexpressible. It involved the universe.

I wrote poems that made no sense, that were addressed

to You. I wrote one each morning, and they came out with force; the poems felt urgent, like messages called out over the ocean during a war.

I am thinking of my English teacher from back then: a "mod" woman, in a short skirt with a chain-link belt around her ample waist; she was too old to dress like that, I remember thinking, but her clothes expressed to me good will, fresh air. She wore purple eye shadow. She was the only teacher in the school who dressed like this, and I sensed that she was an outcast among the staff and that her days were numbered. She was also the only adult who didn't disapprove of me, although she didn't so much express this, as not express disdain; she seemed to regard me respectfully.

She accepted my one poem every morning, which I tore out of my notebook so that the holes were ripped, and it seemed to have come from the middle of nowhere. I remember noticing that sometimes her fingers were stained with ink, when she took my poem; she was a writer too, I thought. She would read my poem seriously and nod, her thin, long hair dipping below her shoulders. And sometimes she would clear her throat, and suddenly begin reading out loud to the class, in a strange, atonal voice, that was both drenched in sadness, yet eerily detached, a voice unlike her normal one, which was very low and confiding. I held my head up in a haughty way while she read, and everyone seemed to stare at me reverentially. But at the same time I remember feeling a certain bewilderment, feeling that I was a scam artist, since I had absolutely no idea what these poems were about, yet she seemed to think I did.

The poems spoke to her, and didn't speak to me, so much as through me.

This was before Watergate, during the Vietnam War, just after Woodstock. Everyone was restless in the school, just waking up. I was just waking up.

I would sit in her classroom with a handful of other students, all of whom, in memory, look somewhat bewildered too. Everyone had long, lank hair. We started out the year disinterested, going through the motions, but then I remember at some point how we began to run to that room, as if it were the only dry shelter left on a slowly sinking ship. Hunkering around an oval table, the days growing long and dark through the windows, we drew in close to hear her better, and to talk. She wore white go-go boots. Sometimes she asked us to write about everyday things: "Describe a color." "Describe what it's like to eat a watermelon." "Describe how it feels to experience the morning." I remember staring at my white paper, as if it were a serene surface of snow where no one had ever walked; I was being asked to express something for the first time in the universe. She would read to us, sometimes from our own writing, sometimes from Kafka, Beat poets, Richard Brautigan. The book *Platero and I*, by Juan Ramón Jiménez, was one of my favorites:

> It was the children's dinnertime. Dreamily the lamp cast its warm pattern on the snow-white cloth, and the red geraniums and red apples added a rough gaiety to that simple idyll of innocent faces. The little girls were eating like grown women; the boys discussed like grown men. In the background, the

> young mother, blond and beautiful, nursing the baby at her white breast, watched smilingly. Outside the garden window the clear starry night trembled cold.

She always read in that haunting way, a lone voice, calling out.

At some point we knew that she would be fired. There were rumors. But there was a general edginess between the administration and all of us, really; it was as if a death threat hung in the air. Some kids began wearing black armbands to protest the war, but the bands seemed fitting in general. Everything we said and read and wrote began to have an urgency about it: the end was drawing near. We never spoke about personal problems, but we knew we were on the brink—of what exactly, we didn't know. The words became more beautiful. She began to smoke in class, pause in the middle of reading to us from *In Watermelon Sugar* and take out a cigarette, which made us crazy with nerves, but awed. She rarely smoked it, but instead kept it lit at her side, like a companion.

Maybe in that dangerous room, if she had asked us to read *The Pigman* it would have been thrilling; we would have set the book in the middle of the room and watched it levitate; we would have come upon it together, like coming upon a new land, or a new color. We had the ability to see things fresh, back then, and it was a fresh book. It might have been wonderful. She would have beheld the book as we did. We never had the feeling that she owned a book.

I remember the morning I ran away from home, when I opened the back door. It was 5:00 a.m. The dawn was quiet; it was spring. I was surprised that the air was so fresh, and the sky was like it used to be, when I was very little, and would wake at dawn and watch the sun rise. The sky was pink that morning, and as I tiptoed out of my yard, I was aware of a huge perceptual shift—a moment of reorientation: like looking out a window and realizing you are not where you thought you were all along. Or being dizzy, and focusing on a point out in the distance that suddenly brings everything else into focus. When I stepped outside, I realized immediately how I had been indoors for so long, unhappy, fretful, walking from room to room, and had been looking down at my feet, at the squares of linoleum in the house, crying, fighting, that the world had shrunk, everything grown small. Stepping out to run away into the pink air surprised me in that I realized I had simply forgotten, or overlooked, the world.

I had left a note on the dishwasher for my mother to find. I copied out lines from *The Prophet,* by Kahlil Gibran:

> *Your children are not your children*
> *They are the sons and daughters of*
> *Life's longing for itself.*

Stars were still out. I ran across town, leaping over curbs, and up hills, to a church, where my boyfriend would be waiting. The church came into view. It appeared awake, and patient. The huge clock on the watchtower looked as if it was drawn in black ink. It, too, was immeasurably calm, a pleasant face against the fading night. I wished the stars would stay. I remember the dew, and how my sneakers got wet, but I liked it.

The library is quiet, the day growing darker from the approaching rain, and I am sleepy, my head still tucked into my arms. A train rumbles by. For a while I doze, although I am aware of the river, and the voices of the librarians, which seem comically loud.

I am so sleepy I decide to stretch out, and take off my shoes. I lower myself onto the floor, between my table and the window, and lie down. Just for a moment. I bunch my sweater up for a pillow. From this position, the library looks upside down. Dust particles float by. I can see the feet of the old man, and am surprised to see he has been wearing loafers all along under the table, big, youthful shoes, although now in his sleep his ankles are tipped outward, and his shoes look much too large for him. I peer up through the slats of his chair, and see that his ears are nearly translucent in the dimming sunlight, and each is rimmed in gold. For some reason, I take this as a good sign.

I used to come to libraries for refuge, when I had nowhere else to go. I drifted through the rooms, spinning the squeaky book rack. I remember when I was twelve, finding *The Stranger,* by Camus, one afternoon, and casually opening it because I liked the title, and reading the first line: "Mother died today, or was it yesterday?"

I wore a green plastic rain poncho—I liked to wear it everywhere; it covered me in a way that made me feel protected, and hip, and gentle. I can picture myself standing by the book rack in that poncho, reading *The Stranger,* feeling that I had never read words hooked together like this, and that something strange and new was happening to me as I read, a feeling that inexplicably conjured an image of formations of white, dazzling quartz, through which can be glimpsed the sea. I read all afternoon, and later slipped the Camus under the folds of my poncho, and stole it. I stole another book also: *A Spy in the House of Love,* by Anaïs Nin.

Everything was alive then, when I was lost: golden rain rushing down curbs under streetlamps, the frail trees. I held on to certain books for safety. I loved *The Crock of Gold,* by James Stephens, *An Episode of Sparrows,* by Rumer Godden.

While I lie on the floor, remembering long ago, a little child runs near me, although he doesn't see me. He is evading his babysitter. He is a green blur. She is chasing him, barefoot, and they are both not saying a word, but she is not enjoying this—and even though he is smiling, I wonder if he is really enjoying himself. I hear her feet thud on the linoleum, and hear her grunt as she runs, and reaches out to grab his arm but misses. Their feet make a thudding sound throughout the library.

I miss Alex and Clair. I picture them in school. Are they OK? Clair wore a shirt with a neat little collar this morning. I have the desire to make a nice meal for them when they come home: potatoes in their "jackets." This is a pleasant thought, and I look up toward the Palisades, which rise up through the windows, and think how beautiful it is now, this time of year, the purple shadows in the rocks, and the trees turning gold, and how this all radiates optimism: nothing bad has happened yet. I picture setting the table, laying the forks on folded napkins.

Chapter Five

Are my children "real troopers"? What exactly do I mean by this?

It used to be a compliment. We used to say it so admiringly, "we" being my friends and I who worked as day-care teachers in the late 1970s, and through the '80s. I bet we, and others in day care, coined the term, at least as applied to children. We said it about the child who'd come through another long day—who was surviving the turbulence of family life, being dropped off at 7:00 a.m. by a parent on his way to work, some who'd already worked a night shift. Or by a single parent, valiant, exhausted, other children in tow, all facing the day. Or by an adult who'd been up all night drinking. The child came down the stairs to the church basement, where the day-care center was located, and stayed there for twelve hours. "But you know what?" we'd say to each other with respect, "Through all this, he's a real trooper." Or, "And who do you think is the strongest of his whole family? (Child's name.)"

A "real trooper" had sass, resilience. He was the opposite of a kvetch, or a child spoiled, or petted, or indulged, or one who was "too sensitive." That was a lily-white octopus of a child, who needed to be toughened up. (Secretly I knew I had been such a child.) A "trooper" didn't cling, didn't talk baby talk, didn't suck his thumb.

I liked working in that day-care center. I allow myself to

stretch out more on the library floor, and remember all those years ago, that cool, damp basement, with no real windows to speak of, but how we struggled to gussy the place up, drape it with yards of cheerful fabric. All those tiny children, some as young as six months old, deposited each morning into a crib with their own box of diapers. And then toddlers, and three- and four-year-olds, up to the fives, who, perhaps in contrast to the rest, always struck me as serious, even somber. The Center was on the Upper West Side of Manhattan, and the kids came from affluent West End Avenue, but also from Harlem, and neighborhoods in between. I had never worked in day care before, but instead had spent time in nursery schools, where children stayed no more than three hours, and then went home to have lunch with their mothers. And I had never been with so many different races, so many rich and poor people intermingled. We celebrated every conceivable holiday linked to every nationality represented, including Kwanzaa, and obscure Jamaican holidays, and Chinese New Year. The commotion, the "diversity" (was that a word we used back in 1978?) felt interesting and vital. It felt *real.*

We wanted to make it feel homey there. A home away from home. We sewed big, red pillows. We had a collage table; we had smooth blocks and tiny cars. Dolls. The staff was warm; we fired officious types who kept their distance. I remember one we fired because she kept showing up for work in white cashmere, which she sought to keep pristine throughout the day. The janitor, a muscular, sweet man named Larry, had swarms of little boys following him while he swept; they imitated his swagger, and each morning when he saw them he'd high-five them, and say, "Yo man! How's my main melon?" The boys beamed.

The cook was big and mean and cranky. But she felt like part of the family too—albeit the scary relative. She wore her bedroom slippers to cook in. It was nerve-racking even to walk by the kitchen, and we all tiptoed when we passed. She made delicious things, things that made your mouth water, grits and Southern-fried chicken and thick apple cake, but if you were lured by the smells to poke your head in, you had to be quiet, lest she see you and raise up her dripping spoon and chase you out. So you stood quiet as a mouse and watched her for only a moment, stirring pots on top of that silver oven, grunting, sometimes muttering to herself. She was an ogre in the same fairy tale we were all living underground.

It was cozy there.

But there was no getting around how long those days were. Each day felt like a double shift, from the child's perspective, that is. (I stayed only eight hours; many of the children stayed on another five.)

"I hate this," I remember a little girl saying one late afternoon. We were sitting outside, on a bench, in the cement playground next to the church. This was our "outdoor period." Near us was a spindly tree, encircled by wire mesh. The sky was white. Some kids were throwing a ball, and a squirrel ran across the tree. I went cold when I heard her say this; she'd said it in a tiny voice, more to herself than to me. She was a delicate Chinese girl; she wore small, black slippers. Her bangs were cut slightly unevenly, on an angle; had she cut them herself?

"What do you hate?" I whispered.

"This," she said, and gestured miserably, and I took it to mean Everything: the endless afternoon, the stupid ball, the same tree. The extended hours of waiting to go home, wanting her mother. The day going on and on.

What had I done, after all, when I was small, in the late afternoon? Certainly not continued to be out in public, still with my shoes on. For me, things began to draw in as the day grew late. I had watched Sandy Becker talk about juicy carrots on TV, and Officer Joe Bolton, who seemed so large and protective, filling up the whole screen in his uniform. He looked me right in the eyes when he spoke. In other words, I had watched TV, lounged on our lumpy couch, night beginning to fall, my mother nearby, starting dinner. It was a quiet time of day, peaceful.

Later that day I ran back inside the Center and begged my colleagues, "We must perk up the late afternoons!" We decided to bring in specialists after four o'clock: new blood, fun. (There seemed to be no end to floating artists back then, looking for work.) We hired a mime, a French teacher, a real gypsy, who whisked the chairs out of the way and handed out scarves for children to dance with to scratchy recordings of Bartok. The lull in the late afternoon, the sleepiness, was turned inside out: we had three more hours to get through, and why not pizzazz them up?

But the little girl's misery threw something into relief for me. Doubts, big doubts, lurked, even amid Bartok, the French chatter, the swirling silk, the last wedges of apple cake. Did we, underground, in the dimming light, really know what the hell we were doing? As kind and sensitive as we strove to be, was it right for such young children to spend their childhoods in these long, slightly orphaned days? What would the ramifications of this situation be? Weren't elemental, inner events taking place during these first days and months and years of small children's lives: a baby first getting a grip on the distinctions between inner and outer reality, for example; feelings of self-worth; the very creation of one's character—shifts and structures as fundamental as the first geologic formations of the universe? And what was so good about children not clinging, not sucking their thumbs? Weren't these expressions of one's desire not to leave, not just yet? Didn't young children have the right to express this? When we admired the troopers, were we celebrating for our own convenience? The trooper was no work, made us feel that we were doing fine; the octopus, on the other hand, was hell. The trooper played us back to ourselves as doing it all right, whereas the unhappy child, who longed for Mother, and peed in his cot at naptime, and showed signs of coming apart at the seams, made the whole day-care thing seem shabby and a failure and wrong.

Just as adults had to work, no kid got a free ride. (Were we starting to think of childhood itself as a "free ride"?) Kids had their job too: Going to Day Care Without Too Much Fuss. And day care was good, better than being alone with just parents; it was *healthy*.

A "real trooper" was something we didn't as often call white children, as I recall, although this was not the sort of observation we would have said out loud to each other. It was never even a thought that came fully into my own consciousness until now, at this long distance; at the time it just hovered on the border. The darker the skin, the more "trooperness" was built in. White children who endured, who didn't complain, who "rolled with the punches" were admired, but in a sense when we admired them, we were seeing them as having blurred their whiteness, gained extra pigment. To the extent that they graduated to being "real troopers" in our estimation, it suggested that they had stepped away from whiteness (read: privilege) toward being darker (read: more of a survivor).

I look through the slats of the library table, I am staring at its underbelly, and at all the tables that thread the room. I am looking for the little boy to make one more swerve through the rows of shelves; I would like to see an actual little child right now. But I do not see him. Instead I see a librarian, a lanky woman, not my sturdy nemesis from Texas. This one is walking swiftly down the row, on flat shoes; she is pumping her elbows. She has her silver hair swept back in a headband, as if she is a large child. The word "goodly" comes to mind. "I'm going out to get a bite," she is calling to someone.

Why am I lying on this dusty floor, under the tangle of table legs? I'm too tired to get up.

Those children in the Center slept on cots at naptime (blue fold-out cots). Naptime was every day from 1:00 to 2:30, like it or not. I would have hated that enforced sleep when I was little.

And how I had loved tiptoeing out of there on my break,

happy I wasn't a child, into fresh air, into rain, into sunshine, to eat flan in a Spanish bodega across Broadway. Away from the restless children and the dank room. I would re-enter the basement after the break, and because there was no natural light down there, and the fluorescent lights were off, the room was simply erased, except for a few white pillows, and shifting bodies. Some children who had never fallen asleep would reach out as I passed, like soldiers desperate for contact in a makeshift hospital, and sometimes I would plow on through, affecting disapproval, since they should have gone to sleep, it was naptime, after all.

But more often I stopped, and sat on the edge of a cot, and chatted quietly with a restless child. I would stroke their hair. Always in the back of my mind was the title of a paper written by Anna Freud about war orphans, called "An Experiment in Group Upbringing"; she had observed that the children who were being raised together in orphanages seemed to use each other as a "group ego," used other children as part of their identity, as a way of feeling whole. When one child left the room, all the others were agitated, uneasy, until the one returned, and they could function again as if they were one organism. In what experiment was I partaking? Was something as big and strange going on here, in the inner lives of these children, something that I couldn't see, that wasn't yet apparent?

Sometimes when I sat on the cot, a child would whisper, "Will you tell 'The Magic Bathtub' after naptime? Please!" It was a story I had started making up one late afternoon, when I felt a general weariness descend in the darkening room, and it had struck me that a story was needed; suddenly only a story would do. I had heard myself calling everyone to drag their little chairs into a circle, and announcing with perfect certainty (that I didn't feel—because I had no idea what I was going to tell) that I would now tell a story, an important story, one I knew well. "Once in New York," I began, and then it was as if I really did know this story, because the story just seemed to roll off my tongue: about two children whose parents had left them, to go to work in Africa (to capture wild animals for the zoo), and who were taken care of by mean babysitters, but the children discovered, "quite by accident," while taking a bath, that by turning the handles on the hot and cold water taps, they could make their bathtub lift off the bathroom floor and fit through the little window and fly. The story just kept telling itself. The two children set sail to find their parents. I remember noticing, after a while, how a soft feeling seemed to sweep through the room, and everyone, even the adults, seemed to relax. I just heard my voice, and I was relaxed too. The children sat in those tiny chairs in a huge circle, around me. I remember their little knees. When I spoke, they seemed brighter, bigger, but more like grown babies than miniature adults.

Sometimes when I sat on the edge of a cot, a child who was begging for the story would reach out and grip my hand. The little hand and the whispered intensity surprised me: Could a story—one I had made up so effortlessly—occupy so important a place in the imagination? Where had that story come from? The tiny hand, and the whispering, and so much feeling, felt intimate. I felt a little shy then; I wasn't used to feeling intimate with individual children in that big room.

Hours later, when my shift was over, I would climb up the stairs again to leave, always into an altered world: night had fallen. Sometimes when I would come up after all those hours underground, I would be shocked to see that it had been snowing, and that the streets were transformed and muted, the car headlights hollow-eyed through drifts.

Was the very paradigm of childhood changing right then too, while I was downstairs, sitting on cots? It was then, in the late 1970s, that most of the problem novels were busily being written. I remember a parent telling me about the books that were being published "now"—about death and divorce, about "latchkey kids"—and me, listening, astounded, really, as she recited those plot lines, before she ascended the stairs on her way to work. Down there in the basement, aside from magic bathtubs, we were reading *Mike Mulligan and His Steam Shovel.*

What trickled down to us from the world above, into that echoey room? In what ways do subtle cultural shifts make themselves felt?

Even though this Center was not part of the Head Start program, we seemed to be inclined to want to "teach" stuff: At staff meetings we asked each other: Why should children wait until first grade to learn to read? Why not earlier, much earlier? (This is more routinely considered now, a generation later, but back then curriculum for very young children did not venture toward reading and writing. That was left until grammar school.) Why not expose children to what's "really" going on in the world? Bringing in "reality" (e.g., "the world is diverse") began to feel in keeping with something modern, urgent, hip.

Didn't we have a speaker come in and talk about the history of the Jews, about the Holocaust, about the founding of Israel, and about the plight of the dislocated Palestinians? An earnest woman with huge silver earrings. The children sat in a semicircle, in those little chairs, their sneakers not quite touching the floor, listening intently, and we felt so righteous in our educating them. (Only later, at snack time, when the children were drinking juice, and I overheard a tiny boy remark happily to his friend, "I like Jews. I like apple Jews, but mostly I like orange Jews," did I begin to wonder at the effectiveness of our adult agenda.)

Suddenly I remember another version of myself, I, the strident day-care teacher, in pursuit of "enriching" the children's education. I press my fingers over my eyes to end the memory, but it looms more vividly.

I can see myself: asymmetrical haircut, one earring, dressed in black. (At what moment, and why, did everyone of a certain age begin to dress increasingly in black?) Marching in one morning with the *New York Times* under my arm as if I had no time to waste, calling the elderly five-year-olds (who suddenly seemed sleepy) around in a circle. "I am going to teach you about what's happening in the world," I said briskly.

(Why oh why couldn't I have just told them about the birth of a new panda in the zoo, or how some baby birds were being helped to survive on a window ledge?)

"Does anyone know what a hostage is?" I said instead. I looked around at the soft, blank faces. "Someone stolen. People can get stolen. And some Americans, that's us, have been taken hostage by Iranians."

I can remember my tone: matter-of-fact, no baby talk, as if conveying, "Look man, Shit Happens. Deal."

This picture of myself, my swinging hair, my black leather bomber jacket, me droning on: it is as if I was momentarily hypnotized, reading from some weird edict that had ordered me to apprise other people's tiny children about international kidnapping. What current had I sailed in on that morning?

I must have been telling myself that this was good for them, it was necessary for children to be informed, reality was empowering, knowledge was power, and so on. I must have been operating with a belief (was I wholly conscious of this thought?) that children were fundamentally on their own in the world, that it was best to equip them with skills for survival.

But to believe this, mustn't I have undergone a shift in my thinking about childhood itself? What about the notion that children needed protection, that they shouldn't have to be faced with huge, adult problems beyond their understanding? What had happened to the certainty that talking of kidnapping and loss and powerlessness and the evil of strangers and the dangerousness of the world would have distinctly different meaning to children than to adults?

Instead, it is as if I had unwittingly marched in that day embodying the culture's new view on childhood: as if I suddenly believed that all children were like adult actors merely playing children.

How else could I have gone on and on like that?

I remember the whole room fell quiet while I spoke, while I described the miseries of the hostages' families, the bravery of Terry somebody-or-other's sister. I remember my fellow teachers standing still, some squeezing blobs of Play-Doh while they listened. But they were all nodding in encouragement at my ranting. Why didn't anybody step forward and whisper in my ear, "You're freaking these kids out!"?

But no one did.

We—adults—must have all been going through some cultural shift of our own just then. Maybe we had been getting used to standing around and listening to terrible stories. Some of us had begun attending Twelve Step programs at night; our very church basement was converted by 8:00 into a meeting place for Adult Children of Alcoholics. We had begun referring to ourselves as "Adult Children." At night in those rooms we sat among strangers and recited the terrible plot lines of our own childhoods. Was the very way we told stories, and the kinds of stories told, changing? A first-person recitation of hell, told by a narrator whose most defining feature was his status as Survivor—was this just coming into vogue?

I picture the room, the blobs of Play-Doh, the little slits of window that let in no light, but which we'd gussied up with red curtains. Like in that old advertisement for weight-loss programs, where a thin person lives inside a fat person, and needs only to be sprung free, it was as if all around me adults were really harboring their inner, aching children. And the actual children, who were expected to bear witness to stories of atrocities same as the rest of us, were furiously sucking their thumbs, harboring, inside their child bodies, full grown adults. As overgrown kids, we had a need to smack something full in the faces of these putative children: Reality.

I remember I pulled out an ultrasized calendar we used for marking down birthdays and for teaching the days of the week, and dramatically selected a red crayon, and then proceeded—while everyone watched, children and adults alike—to mark off the roomy boxes with huge irate X's, denoting the days gone by when Americans were still being held hostage.

And it was only when a child began to cry, and then another asked politely, "Who's going to steal us today?" and other children grew fidgety with anxiety and began bulleting around the room, that I was shaken out of my stupid, adolescent, postmodern idea of children, still holding the crayon in midair. The adults shrank back into their own skins, and the children looked very, very small, and I finally shut up.

The memory of my stridency, my insensitivity, makes me roll under the library table today. I am ashamed. Under here the network of slats is lined with soothing pavilions of dust, thick as suede.

The old man is shifting in his seat, having woken, and I can hear him swallowing. He stands. I hear his bones creak. His big, youthful loafers still do not fit him as well as he is pretending. There is a lagoon of space between his foot and the shoe. I shut my eyes, but I can feel the precise moment when he sees me. He is staring. Is he wondering if something is terribly wrong with this woman on the floor?

But he doesn't raise a fuss, and although I keep my eyes closed, I continue to feel him looking down at me. He is hesitant to leave me. "It looks like rain," he whispers finally, but he isn't expecting a reply; his comment is merely informative, an old man informing the dead. I do not answer. I hear him creak away.

I am safely hidden under the table. The darkness of the afternoon is pillowlike through the glass. The trees are swaying. I think of flying, of a billowing shower curtain, made of satin. The darkness of the afternoon under the table feels comforting. I doze.

The librarians are talking so loudly I feel indignant. I think about shouting, "Uh, do you mind? This is a library! I'm trying to get some sleep!" Luckily I realize the folly of this, and I stop myself.

I sit up. I am surprised to see that the librarian, the first one, is walking softly along the periphery of the room, as if waiting for her shadow to lead the way. She is drawing the shades, pulling delicate cords.

I sink back down between the table and the window. I must have dozed again, because this time when I open my eyes she is standing over me, and so is the other one—the goodly one, whose velvet headband sweeps her hair back; in my mind I call her Alice. She and I have never spoken, but I have noted over the years that she always seems to be wearing a smock. Her blue eyes are vivid, mischievous.

I casually wipe drool from my chin.

"Reading does this to some people," says Alice.

"Hi," I say weakly.

The sturdy one in her Texas accent explains about me. "She's been reading the 'Doom and Gloom' books." To me she adds, "That's what we call them."

Alice replies, "Oh—my mother's boyfriend raped me, and my mother is in jail, and I have a brain tumor? Those books?"

I study them. They don't seem hostile in the least. Have I misjudged them? Are they regarding me as someone sent from a central agency, long awaited? Sent to the outposts to hear their gripe?

I sit up properly and make to slap dust off my legs, as if this lying position had been foisted on me, and is infinitely irritating. In one swoop I am a citizen, sitting upright. I stand, and to distract them from my dustiness, and the eggshells and wrappers that litter the table, I say, loudly, "I have realized what is missing in those books."

They wait expectantly.

"Open destiny."

They continue to stand expectantly, and I struggle to remember what it is I am referring to, and then I do.

"It's from a line in a Grace Paley story. She describes how she hates stories that move from point a to point b, toward an ending that's fixed before starting out. You know, contrived. She says she hates that absolute line between two points"—and then I lower my voice, and recite—"'. . . not for literary reasons,' she says, 'but because it takes all hope away. Everyone, real or invented, deserves the open destiny of life.'"

They are nodding.

"I've always preferred open destiny myself," Alice says.

Before we can continue, the bank of lights overhead has been turned out, and then another bank. I realize there has been a third librarian all along, a frail Indian woman in a sari. The room is blue now, and through the blinds, lightning crackles in the sky, although as far as I can tell, it is not yet raining.

"We close early today," Alice says. The two women have a few last-minute things to do. They walk quickly to the front desk. I sit for a minute in the shadowy room, with the wide, darkening sky beyond, wondering if I should run home right now, or wait for the inevitable storm to pass.

But then the rain begins, and with it I feel a surge of sadness, as if something has been taken from me. I watch the rain dimple the river, and the clouds rumble by. I can smell the metallic rain.

The old man who has been reading near me all morning is standing under the roof outside, with his newspaper over his head. The newspaper is perfectly creased, like a delicate Chinese sun hat. His ears are no longer lit. The child who had been running around stands out there also, now holding on to his babysitter's leg; he looks fearful of the storm, and she is shielding him.

I decide to wait inside. Through the window I watch the reflection of the darkening season, the racing river, the wet trees glowing through the glass. But except for the hammering of rain, everything is quiet.

Chapter Six

One fine, clear day, long ago, back when I was new in town, I was driving around to get someplace—where exactly I no longer remember—and after a time admitted to myself that I was lost. I pulled down an unfamiliar dead-end street, into a driveway, so I could turn around and try again. I remember feeling quite upset; perhaps I was late. I yanked the car in reverse, and was on the verge of tears, when I happened to glance up at the house at the end of the driveway. Something about the house arrested me, I can think of no better word, and I stopped.

It was a peeling, white house, and for whole moments while I simply gaped at it, a bad feeling washed over me, bad but good too: this was a familiar house, I recognized this house, this house had my fingerprint on it. It wasn't so much that I knew this house exactly, but something in it, or about it. The house was turned slightly away from its own driveway, so I was seeing it as if in profile; it offered mostly a shabby, white side, like the shoulder of someone daydreaming in another room, who hasn't yet glanced over. Long, small-paned windows enclosed the front, and the effect was poetic, but the roof was sagging, and the color of the door had long since worn off, although it was possible to tell it had once been red. The yard, lit up in the bright sun, was muddy, rutted with dozens of haphazard footprints. Later, I would find out this place had been a rental for thirty years, with constantly changing tenants, but the fact that it was a neglected house was obvious: neglected, yet brimming with faint good humor. What I experienced, as I sat in the driveway, was a strange mixture of recognition, and aversion, as in "Oh no, not this again."

This is the house we now live in. It turned out that about a year after this first sighting, we discovered we had to move suddenly, and the house in question was the only available rental in town. My heart sank when this all fell into place, although I wasn't totally surprised. The house is needy. The ceilings are high, but the rooms are tiny and confusing. Big windows face west, and at four o'clock, the living room is saturated with brilliant light. But everything needs repair, everything, although we feel sometimes that, beneath the wreck, a realer, more beautiful house dwells.

What I found most unsettling about living here was the muddy yard. Only the frailest path lay between yard and street. Neighbors were in the habit of using the yard for nightly games of catch, and even though they stopped when we moved in, I sensed that the house continued to be regarded as public property. At night, especially, I felt exposed. Finally, last year, we bought the house, and installed a fence, a white picket fence, with a latched gate, and now I feel better. We planted some grass where the rutted footprints were, and a small garden. The fence follows the slight hilliness of the land, and gently disrupts the flow of past and present.

Now, in the autumn, the fence is draped with yellowing vines; now the garden has collapsed. I put a mirror up on the wall of the porch, so that it reflects the windows opposite it, and thus creates the illusion of itself as a window. In the mirror, leaves drift, lazy but insistent. There are no red leaves out there; all the falling leaves on our street are yellow, a green-yellow, the color of Anjou pears.

Clair comes up the stone path, singing to herself. Her cheeks are a high color, and her hair is somewhat wild; she is in the second grade. She is very tall, the tallest in her class. "Hi Mommy!" she is calling. She runs now that she has seen me, her blue knapsack bouncing, her hair streaming, and hugs me, and is handing me a two-page note. I read the first page:

"You are invited to hear the children's memoirs. They have been working very hard. Please help us celebrate their completion! Tuesday, 10:00 a.m."

Something strikes me as comical about this, and when I look up I expect to see Clair as a little middle-aged woman (which is hard, as she is jumping up and down). How does a seven-year-old go about writing a memoir? And why?

"What are your memoirs about?"

"About you," she says, and when she strokes my shoulder, it is with an air of sadness, as if she knows something unfortunate about my fate. Then she skips off.

The sun is at a brilliant, late-afternoon pitch, lighting up my little garden, which is right by the front door. There are only bright marigolds in the leaves now; all the other flowers have died. But at the height of the summer, not so long ago, really, my garden was jam-packed—great stalks of blue hollyhocks, white hibiscus, yellow gladioli. Everything grew tall. In between the stalks were small flowers—lily of the valley, velvety leaves—which I had put there with half a mind that Clair might want to bring her dolls over and let them traipse under the stalks. The low and the high seemed like something that might appeal to her.

But it didn't. Pointing to the fragrant, cool underside, I asked her more than once: "Don't you think your dolls would like to have a little picnic there?" Each time, she would stop—she always seemed to be clomping, wearing a pair of my old high heels—and would say, "It's pretty there." But then she would resume her onward clomping.

And she would go behind a crab apple tree, which is where she has gone now, her favorite place to play. I watch her as she settles into a bunch of yellowing weeds, carefully laying an apple and some cookies down onto the grass. I can see her perfectly. In the summer I wouldn't have been able to make her out this clearly, since then the place was obscured by a dense screen of Queen Anne's lace. I would only be reminded she was there if I caught a glimpse of a bright sleeve. Now, however, the flowers are frail, and here she is. She is obviously deep in play. Her head is tilted in conversation. She might be singing a little.

I haven't ventured over there much, so today as I cross the crunchy grass—I want to ask her more about her memoirs—I am interested to see how overgrown it really did get here. The dying forsythia make a low wall of sorts, and the smooth yellow-green leaves drifting down through the branches are feathering the enclave as if it were its own little forest. There are late roses. It is the western part of the yard, and the light is strong, highlighting the veins in the leaves.

I poke my head in. "Hi, Clair."

She looks up, absolutely startled. "How'd you find me?" she gasps.

Now it's my turn to be startled. Could it be that she really believes she's totally hidden? Can the illusion be that powerful that when you play, you are *gone?*

"A lucky guess," I say. "Aren't you cold sitting there?"

Her cheeks are bright from the wind, a robust little girl, who does not look cold in the least. She is staring at me intently, as if she is trying to make up her mind to confide something.

"What is it?"

In a very solemn voice, but very clear because this low chamber of hedges seems to block out all other sounds, she makes a statement: "Roses *are* prettier than Queen Anne's lace." I wait to hear more, but she has shut her mouth, as if—*there,* she's said it. Now she is studying me closely. Little faces of maroon roses are peering at me smugly. From her tone, and demeanor, it seems what she has stated is the final conclusion of some lengthy debate. She studies my face for a response, which I sense is best given as a nod, showing that I have registered the fact.

I have had a window into her play, only the view is deeply mysterious. Walking back to my own side of the yard, I have a sudden, fleeting memory of what it felt like being a child, to feel as if you were a citizen in two places at once: the everyday world and then *over there,* which was just to the side, where everything was vivid in a different way—colors deeper. Entry involved a quick leaping over a stripe of bright water. What I wanted most was to return to that place and drink in my deep thoughts.

"Your child's classroom" (I read on the second page of Clair's note) "has been selected to host weekly visits from a writing specialist, sent from Teachers College! Your child will receive critique on all aspects of writing, and learn how to edit, re-write and publish! Children will be expected to Write, Write, Write!"

I stare at this note for a long time. Finally I sit on a rock.

Why does this child—whom I can see through the weeds, who seems to be making a solemn pledge, her hand raised—why does this ardent child need an expert between her and the written word? Just yet? Why would a seven-year-old—who is just learning to write, who tells me that she loves to pretend that all the letters are alive, that M is the meanest because its eyebrows meet in the middle—need critique? Now? Need to edit and rewrite, to look backward, critically, when it seems she ought instead to be plowing ahead? Aren't revising, polishing, publishing a gamut of activities meant for adults? Or maybe adolescents?

A lumpy worm is lit, the same rosy gold, and he slithers between the dead stalks. All summer I battle my disgust of worms, reminding myself that they are the true tillers of the soil (and never quite buying the whole idea), but now, in the sun, even he seems kingly, going about his purposeful life. What life has he made underneath? He dips into a hole in the earth and vanishes. A remark of Picasso's seems apt: "The presence of what is erased still glows," he said.

Wasn't the act of erasing very strange, nearly magical, long ago, in second grade? Wasn't erasing back then a calamity of sorts?

I remember facing a wrong, misshapen letter, and the rubbing and rubbing, and the crumbs, the inevitable hole in the paper, and smudging. Something just a bit mean about getting rid of the letter, just because it was weak. But then I never felt that I got anything off the paper, so much as pushed it inside. Paper, having that capacity to open and shut, swallowed the rejected letter, all with a straight face, unbeknownst to any adult onlooker.

But then no adult onlooker asked us to rewrite back then. No experts back then. Our erasing came when we'd misspelled only, or got a wrong answer. Those teachers in elementary school were sometimes stern, bossy, but remote too, when we wrangled with the first acts of writing; they stayed far off in the front of the room, at their desks. They had merely passed on a very ancient system, one which predated them. They just told us what to write about, to be neat, what rules to follow when we wrote. Which they responded to with a hearty check or some irate cross-outs. Maybe a spare comment. But no more.

Which left just me, just the paper, the pencil, the mystery of words, all of which seemed to have secret compartments. This was enough. I liked this distance. I liked how my teachers didn't comment too much, just handed back the papers with a few checks or cross-outs.

In fact, this silence elevated them in my estimation; it felt significant. I read into it a permissiveness, an expression of a certain grace, never seen otherwise during the school day: "Make your own way," their silence seemed to say. "This is what all human beings must do."

After a while, I fold up the note from Clair's school, tucking away the idea of a writing consultant who will help Clair edit and publish her memoirs. Perhaps, I realize suddenly, most people would be happy—thrilled—that their child was to receive so much attention from experts about her relationship with words. Maybe something interesting and wonderful will happen. Am I crazy to feel uneasy at the idea of these extra services? I stand up.

Only a small sinking feeling remains, but mostly I am curious. What will this "memoir celebration" be like?

Story Shop is an after-school program I run for children, which, as I explain to parents, "helps children find forms for their original stories." Children write stories, and tell them, and enact them, and build scenes and characters out of paper and boxes and odds and ends. Stories are often presented to the group as a whole, so that kids get a chance to share what they've made, and also to draw inspiration from the work of others.

I began Story Shop when Alex was little, and I needed a part-time job that would allow me to work close to home. For the previous ten years I had been teaching writing as an adjunct professor in colleges, and while I liked this, what I loved most was working with children, especially in the arts, and especially as it gave me a chance to be in the realm of childhood imagination. I had been a teacher of writing for children in many different venues: in a residential treatment center for emotionally disturbed children, in a fantastically wealthy private school, and as part of an arts program in a low-income neighborhood. I had loved these jobs. When I look back at my invention of Story Shop—it began with just a few kids, and has grown steadily—it makes sense to me that I created a situation for myself where I could land right back in that favorite realm. Now I run Story Shop out of a rented room in a church that faces the river. I hold classes for different ages. Story Shop begins at four o'clock.

Today is the first class of the year. I set out crayons. I set out hoops of tape, a sack of fabric. The group that will arrive today, eleven-year-olds, is the group I have known the longest: since they were three. These kids were members of the first Story Shop I ever ran, when they were tiny, and I barely knew what I was doing. They have simply stayed on, year after year, and I have known them, thus, throughout the span of their childhoods. I am thinking of Emily as I set out paints and paper: a delicate girl whom I regard as the lightning rod for the group, the group's narrator, who tips me off, it seems, in clear single sentences, as to the group's deepest wishes. This dates back even to when she was three, a girl with very short bangs and a clear, bright voice that seemed to rise above the other voices.

Now she rushes in, her arms stretched out, and orbits like a plane: "I'm home!" she cries. "Story Shop! Finally!"

She has grown tall over the summer, beautiful. She still wears bangs, but they are longer now. I see the contours of high cheekbones that I have not noticed before. There is a sparse sprinkling of acne on her lively face; she is wearing green nail polish, has a ring with a yin-yang design on her pointer finger. A preteen. This group will now be different, it dawns on me. In this year, when these kids will turn twelve, some change must be on the horizon; Story Shop is in for a change of sorts too, although what the nature of these changes might be, I do not know. What will Emily explain to me now, in this pivotal year?

"I need a refrigerator box this year," she is saying seriously. "I want to sit in it."

I think: "Oy. Where could I store a refrigerator box?"

She says, "It's the only thing I want, a place like that to sit in."

"OK," I say uncertainly.

The others come: ten of them. We hug. We eat. We talk. I have brought cookies.

While we chat, a happy feeling radiates through me, a feeling I never remember until we are all together. Someone has brought a jar of pickles—our tradition.

I remember the very first Story Shop, years ago: little strangers sitting on a magenta blanket, studying me with very clear eyes, while I spoke. I had planned to simply tell a story, and then invite them to tell or draw stories back. But when I was done, one child—Emily—whose name I didn't yet know, jumped to her feet and said "Could we just put this blanket on the table?" The whole group looked back to me, wide-eyed, as if, I remember feeling, they had come in not as a group of children who'd never met (which was the case) but as a committee who had planned beforehand to make this request, as if all over town they'd been trying to get some grownup to drape a blanket over a table, and I was their last shot. Emily spoke in her bright voice, which was very high: "We want to make a nest," she explained.

Years later we still talk about those early days. I tell them about draping that blanket, how they made nests under there. "When I was close to you," I sometimes tell them, "I could hear your stories."

"What were they about?"

"Mommy birds going out to find food, a wolf sneaking around, danger. Baby birds taking naps. The mommy feeding the babies. Babies crying when the mommy left. Things like that. And Cathy took the crayons and paper in the nest and drew a picture I still remember: a little spot of red, a little spot of yellow, and a little spot of green. Then she told me a story to go with the spots."

"What was my story?" Cathy asks, charmed by her younger self. She already knows the answer that I relay:

Red goes away.
Yellow goes away.
Green goes away.

I remember myself, slightly befuddled as to what my role was: everyone under the table, yakking on, chirping, busy without me. If I went under there with them, I felt a bit as if I was imposing, although they seemed glad enough to have such a large visitor. But wasn't I supposed to be guiding them somehow? While I stood beside the table, fretting, handing over bits of paper to serve as worms, I was all the time overhearing those early stories, told in tiny voices, and knew also that I would miss the whole fragile thing if I insisted they just come out already, pay attention, and learn something or other. Sometimes at the end of the hour I would go in—it was kind of humid in there—and I would tell the stories I'd been overhearing: "Once there was a mommy and a little nest of chicks . . ."

"What do you remember?" I've asked them over the years.

"The only thing I remember was that Josh always wanted to be a weak bird—"

"Remember in the winter when we made people from snow? Old men and a witch. And we got a cigar from somewhere, and we lit it, and you could see the orange tip, and it was snowing—"

"That was much later, when you guys were about eight," I point out.

"Remember that play Emily and Anna did about a girl in a haunted house who kept thinking everything that brushed against her was just her little brother trying to scare her? But it was really real ghosts and murderers and vampires? And she kept knocking them over? Because she was so sure they weren't real? But they were real."

It's interesting what remains in memory.

Now we are sitting at the table, which is by the window; the river glitters through the trees. It is as if we have never quite stopped talking, all summer, and are picking up where we left off, although—is there a touch of a new shyness among us? All the girls, not just Emily, seem to have slightly changed their outlines; occasionally I get a glimpse of a new presence within, although only for a moment, and then it slips back, and nothing has changed. The boys, on the whole, seem less on the brink, more one with themselves.

The children's conversation is about the summer, school, new pets, *Harry Potter,* and other beloved books: *The Golden Compass,* by Philip Pullman ("awesome"); *Holes,* by Louis Sachar; Garfield and Calvin and Hobbes comics. They discuss an annoying girl in school who copies answers. No one looks at each other while speaking; they never really have. Instead, they draw while talking, they interrupt each other. Boys and girls in other settings don't talk together too much, I gather, but here they do. "We don't hate boys as much in Story Shop," Emily explained once.

I listen while they chat. The table is littered with colorful papers, ink. The river light washes over us, but the fluorescent bulbs overhead are weak. It is not well lit in here, and this used to bother me, and I would drag in the old lamps from another room, but these too had low-wattage bulbs. Then sometime, long ago now, I came to realize that this lack of bright light was not necessarily bad. To speak in a small group, where there is low light, and also no introduction, no summation, no headline, is like writing in invisible ink: a secret is present but vanishes the instant it is revealed. Yet it hangs in the air, its meaning lingers, it is shared in memory.

Story Shop had been going on for a couple of years, and children had continued making up stories, telling them, writing, drawing, and acting them out, all inspired by their play. But often I felt as if I was still standing outside the nest, wondering: What can I contribute? How ought I to shape this? What structures can I provide that do not intrude? Then, one day, I made an important discovery. It was through remembering something, which in turn reminded me of how the imagination is linked to the idea of miniature.

I was six, standing in a drugstore with my father, and saw four tiny toy chairs hanging in a clear packet from a display rack. My father agreed to buy them for me. I ripped them free and held them, one at a time, in my palm. They were made of a thick, nearly rubbery plastic, but delicate, their legs tapered to points, as sharp as little needles, and their backs straight, broader at the top, and gradating in slightly at the waist. They were the size of my pinky. They were pink like bubble gum, but a shade browner. Maybe it was the first time I'd seen plastic—at least plastic in a casual, cheap toy. I turned the chairs over and over looking for seams, some indication of how they had been put together, and saw the tiny word "Japan" printed in raised letters, underneath their seats, which added to their allure. Other than this word, they had no texture whatsoever.

That night, I found a cardboard box and placed the chairs carefully in a little circle. And it was this sudden feeling that gripped me: Something real was present in the box; here was a secret house, which I was in charge of, a house within my own house, but this one my parents didn't know about. It dawned on me—as it dawns on virtually all children at some moment in their lives—that I could use things to make other things, and in this case, I could, for example, clip tiny images from magazines, to hang as art on the cardboard walls. I was charmed that the tiny chairs cast their own shadows, and each time I left and came back, I felt that someone had just been, a moment before, sitting in the chairs. Once or twice I wondered if it might be the chairs themselves that were alive, since they seemed to be made of flesh.

Upon remembering this, something fell into place, and I suddenly understood how to proceed in Story Shop. The next day I brought in a few boxes I found in my closet. The children gathered around. Word spread: "She's got boxes!" It was as if I had finally, finally, brought food from their native land. They descended on the boxes with vigor and a kind of know-how that edged me to the outskirts: a tribe clearly at home. Everybody started to make things out of other things, and this opened up a new and to this day persistent component of Story Shop: collecting junk (sea glass, keys, old envelopes, doorknobs, broken yo-yos, etc.), transmuting junk, dreaming junk. Wallace Stevens asks, "Is it the philosopher's honeymoon one finds on the dump?" and I know the answer. The junk goes in the boxes, transforming them into scenes from stories, moods, places where stories take place. I estimate I have carted over one thousand boxes to date; sometimes my car has been so crowded with boxes that they ride on my lap, hook onto my elbows as I drive. "What a child wants most is to create a world in which to find a place to discover a self," Edith Cobb writes, and if this is so, then the box, the lowly box, is all a human child really needs.

Today, sitting in this waning October light, among these large preteens, I describe their assignment, "if you should care to accept"—I always add. It is a variation on what I have now been saying for years: "Create a place where a story happens. This can be in a box, or"—I add—"anywhere in the room: under the table, behind the closet door, behind the radiator, anywhere. Use the stuff we have"—which today seems to be blankets, sheets, lights, umbrellas, along with the miniature junk— "then," I finish up, "make the story that goes on in that place."

The sun sinks. The room is filled with that soft light. There is the sound of scissors, flashes of cloth, furniture moving.

Mark, a boy who is more silent than the others, who has a still, angular face, and whose most expressive feature is his wild hair, like an upsweep of dry sea grass, has lugged over an electric fan. He asks if he can use it, and I tell him of course.

"I'll be out here, if you need me," I call, and some look up and wave. The kids like it when I leave, and then come back later, so they can surprise me with all they've done. I quietly close the door into the hall.

This is an old church, lovingly cared for, its stone floor polished, the brass banister gleaming. The small kitchen is tidy too; a dishrag is folded precisely in half, and hangs over the faucet. I peer into the quiet cupboard, as I often do, and take down the old cookie tin, whose bright snowy lid is pried off with some difficulty. Then I go out into the living room, where I sit on a small, flat couch, to wait.

The children and I refer to this room as The Green Room, because of the faded green carpet, in which I now see tracks left by an invisible vacuumer. Pushed to the side, under a window, are two black trunks I bought at a discount store long ago; in there are stored children's stories and drawings. There are some old sculptures also, pushed against the walls, lost in the shadows for now. Sometimes children come in here and open these archival trunks, look over old stuff. They come into this room when they want to make up plays, to stretch out without shoes on, to do somersaults.

The cookie I have stolen is a butter cookie. Through the windows, as I eat, I watch a spire of rising smoke. The days are growing shorter. A slow barge glides across the distant river, its lights casting a watery glow. The river is turning black. "You are our captain," Emily said once.

I am happy. I hear laughter through the wall, lighthearted laughter. I hear the screeching of a table being shoved. They are remaking the whole world in there, taking matters into their own hands.

"We love to pretend we're orphans now," Emily tipped me off one day, back when they were nine or so. "Not the sad part of orphans, just the free part." I think of this now as I hear them shoving tables over in the other room: Free orphans are in that room, shoving tables.

When they were very young, three or four, their stories certainly were not about orphans. Their stories were strange, more like dreams, about being lost, about every new thing emerging out of every thing before it: "Then the cat became the dog." "Then the father was the moon." And on and on, huge stories told not so much by narrators as by wide-eyed witnesses.

Until some time in third grade, it seemed. At which point many became cheerful orphans, who were no longer merely eyes in a dream, but solid narrators, solid main characters, agents of action. This has been so for a long time now; the span of middle childhood is very long. Being orphans seems to be a central organizing fantasy now.

The lights are wobbly on the river, and the barge makes its steady, graceful progression onward, and is growing smaller; the night is looming. What is their nature, these spontaneous orphan stories of middle childhood?

I fling open the lid of an old trunk; it is deep with papers. I sort through heaps.

"I am going to teach you about the Millenius orphans," I read from a story (written in large, loopy script) by a rather stately eleven-year-old girl:

"The oldest was Julienne of 10, who kept them organized. She kept a daily log. The other two were Sean and Bobbina, who had both turned eight recently. Sean was their protector, who would go on their daily raids. Bobbina was the one who did more subtle chores, such as cleaning and cooking and sewing . . ."

And so it is in nearly all these stories from the trunk: parents are dead, and the children are self-sufficient pioneers.

And what else can be said? I read randomly. Many plots involve orphans (or lone, slightly odd characters about seventeen years old) on an adventure, who discover—through luck or magic or sheer ingenuity—just the right tools for survival; who are in search of something, often some kind of treasure, but just as likely a secret door, or hidden passageway; who encounter talking animals, fairies, witches, kings, "bad guys"; and who on their adventures are surprised (delighted) to find that they themselves have access to magic. A character—usually the orphan adventurer—finds he can fly, or disappear, breathe under water, shrink, and the like. Even in stories that begin more "realistically"—for example, a boy being woken by his mean uncle in the morning—magical aspects are part of the mundane: the boy can jump over the wall to get to his uncle fast, so he won't be yelled at for being late.

The kids seem always to have an easy time making up their stories. I picture them chatting, snipping—but at the end of the hour unfurling huge (not always written down, but recited) intricate narratives, quite complete. "Set down with hardly any effort," as Nabokov describes creating, and remembering creating, in his own childhood.

The energy in so many stories is resilient, dynamic, each day brimming with promise.

"Viviane Cobbler" by a nine-year-old girl, is written in bold, purple magic marker:

> Out came Viviane Cobbler tumbling through the door followed by Mrs. Gibbs.
>
> "And never come back!"

> Viviane Cobbler was selling pies: apple pie, blueberry pie, pumpkin pie and cherry pie. Each pie cost one dollar. She hadn't sold one single pie, not even her famous cobbler.
>
> Viviane had no home, nor did she have a mother. She slept in a haystack near a barn, near Old Quicker Street. She loved to watch the horses. Her favorite horse was Scamp. He was a stallion. Viviane watched the riders everyday. She knew exactly how to ride. She always wished she could someday ride Scamp.
>
> She imagined herself riding in a field, galloping over fences.

An entrepreneurial orphan who tumbles on the page, who knows "exactly how to ride"! What is freed in the soul by the orphan fantasy? What accounts for the vibrant energy that accompanies so many orphan stories and games?

It must have to do in part with the way the fantasy takes the child into so potentially terrifying a realm, and then lets him emerge unhurt. To pretend one is an orphan is to willfully enter the scariest childhood fantasy, namely being all alone in the world. To then be able to flip the terror into triumph, where one can cast oneself as not in the least afraid, or lonely, or wanting, but as self-sufficient, and highly powerful, is exhilarating indeed.

And it is as if by killing off one's parents, one becomes flush with his own inexhaustible power to create everything for himself.

So many stories I sift through now hum with this exuberant power of being able to make things up, and make things happen, and just make things. The stately eleven-year-old girl writes from the point of view of a bird: "Jeremiah soared away from the nest he had been confined to for so long. He gave a great flap, and he saw the whole woods lain out before him. It felt great to be a falcon at this point in life. He was old enough to depart his parents, and he was exercising his power to fly where he pleased."

"Suddenly, as if they were made of wax," I read from a story by an eleven-year-old boy, and in this sentence I feel the presence of the orphan's power, "three chairs and a heavy oak table molded themselves out of thin air and fell to the floor right where Gertrude had imagined them to be."

Do problem novels, with their attention to lone and lonely children in dire conditions, capitalize on this naturally occurring fantasy in childhood, namely to be a self-reliant, free orphan? Do they piggy-back in?

But what about children who are in dire conditions, who are truly bereft? (Some children I have known can barely make up anything because they are too overwhelmed by troubles.) I pace around as I ponder this. I nab another cookie from the kitchen. What about children who might be deeply troubled, but who are free enough for the moment to create? Does the zesty, magical creative energy uniquely available to this age prevail? What kind of stories do they make up?

In the trunk I spy a little pencil drawing of a cat, with small ears and dainty paws, and lift it out. I remember the sad girl who drew it. I walk over to the window to try to see the cat better in the light of the setting sun, but the cat is not much illuminated. It was barely drawn, pencil faint.

She was an interesting girl, around nine when I last saw her. She has since moved away. Mother distant; a string of babysitters. A lone child. Clothes too small. Shiny eyes, sparkly, but lone.

I remember her on the floor, mewing a bit (lots of kids have mewed in Story Shop), but she wound herself around my ankles, and it startled me when she whispered, "We are all your orphans."

I felt a freaky coldness when she said this. I feel it a bit now too as I stand by the window, holding the cat; in the pale light I notice for the first time a single strand of hair scotch-taped on the corner of the paper. Why did she do this?

I think of the snowy night of "The Little Match Girl," the saddest story of my childhood, about a girl so poor and alone that she dies in the cold, selling matches. It was such a haunting story to me as a child: the last story on the last night of the world. A story about how loneliness and hunger can eat you up. It didn't end, so much as dissolve. I feel this same hopelessness in the ghostly outline of the poor cat: he is about to fade off.

But I don't remember the girl's stories—she enacted them dramatically—as sad. Everyone was quiet on the periphery of the room while they watched her shows. She played every part: the rich British lady with the twirling umbrella, the butler, then the cat whom the butler finds out in the rain. Everyone liked her shows. The kids were very still while they watched. She seemed radiant when she was done. After kooky twists of plot, the cat—tricky in his own way—was always adopted. In one version, didn't she play him walking with a swagger, twirling the umbrella himself, and in a voice that seemed to have the jaunt of Mae West, asking, "Hey, how does an orphan get along in this town? I don't even have a watch."

I like remembering this. The maudlin aura of "The Little Match Girl" and this poor pencil cat recedes. It seems significant that she chose not to tell her sad story sadly; sadness seems not to be grappled with head-on in middle childhood. (In adolescence things are different.) The girl planted her hidden wish in the beautiful country of her story, and then granted her wish. A writer can plant wishes in stories and grant them, all unbeknownst to the reader.

The orphans shoving tables in the other room are flush with a certain vigor unique to their moment in childhood. None of them would ever settle for the Little Match Girl, for her passivity. They would steal before they would let themselves waste away. Their spirit is hearty; they are like pirates.

If we were all on the river barge I'm watching, which now is a glowing speck in the distance, everything lost would be welcomed aboard: each fallen ticket, lost key, delicate seashell. Each object that finds a home in Story Shop is like an orphan, hoisted up, welcomed aboard.

For a moment, in the dark room, I long to hear my own children's voices. I call home on the church telephone. Alex answers. It is delightful to hear him. He is breathless with excitement.

"Hi, Mom! Guess what! Remember I told you Mel Brooks was in preproduction to make the play version of *The Producers?*"

"Uh, sure." (I sort of remember.)

"You can buy tickets starting next week! I just saw it in the paper!"

"Oh, great!"

"Ma! Can we go? It's going to be so good!" In a lower voice, "I don't want to bother you, but it will probably be so great. Mel Brooks wrote the book and the lyrics too! It's based on his movie, you know that, right, Mom? And Nathan Lane is in it! You like Nathan Lane! I have some money saved up. Can we?"

"We'll think about it—"

"Ma, we should hurry, I think; I think the tickets will sell out—"

"Sweetheart, they won't sell out, believe me. I don't think it will be so popular to the general public as it is to you. There's no rush. But we'll see after Story Shop and we'll talk about it more then. We have plenty of time."

"Story Shop is almost over," I call from the doorway. The room is a carnival of intriguing structures.

Ten children have made ten stories, each intricate and quirky, and everyone gathers to hear each other's tales, and witness their stage sets. Mark, the boy with the expressive hair, has made a story using the electric fan, which he flips on to begin telling his story. Attached to the fan is one thread, now whipping around. "This," he begins, pointing to the thread, "is a man rushing to the dentist. This is all you can see of the man, since he's running so fast." Everyone is engrossed, listening.

Only Emily is not here. She is under a table, which she has draped with cloth.

"I really need it," she whispers from under there, when I lift up the cloth.

"What?"

"The refrigerator box!"

"What's the matter?" I whisper through the flap.

"I don't need to be spoken to right now," she whispers back.

How am I to understand this? Is her desire to hide an expression that something is wrong? Or am I witnessing a desire merely for a cocoon, so she can evolve in private? In some sense the child, and the adolescent also—I recall the words of psychoanalyst D. W. Winnicott—does not want to be found "before being there to be found."

Later, when Story Shop is over, and everyone has gone, I look under the table and see she has left behind a page on which she drew six ovals, each topped with a different hairstyle. But each oval is blank; each is a face, waiting to be drawn.

What change is upon us?

Alex's language arts teacher this year is a young man, a self-described poet, who has shiny thick hair, cut like James

Joyce's, with Joyce's wire spectacles too. He has a sense of humor, although it is only suggested by the slight upturn of his lips sometimes. Alex likes him, and he likes Alex. He apparently likes the way Alex writes poetry, and tells him, "Poetry is your unit, man!" Alex reports this as amusing, for reasons we never discuss. Sometimes when I have nothing particular to say to Alex, when he is lying around on the couch, I exclaim from the doorway, "Poetry is your unit, man!" He smiles marginally.

But best of all, this teacher has admitted that he isn't crazy about some of the books they have to read, sees them as "poor quality" and too gloomy. But he has no choice he says, they are decided by the English committee. He doesn't evidence any critique of the books, however; he still issues tests on them, and Alex's first assignment was to make a poster listing the symbols in *Chasing Redbird,* and their corresponding referents (e.g.: dog = trust; trail in woods = Zinny finding herself). But his teacher's disaffection with the books gives Alex a bit of breathing room, I think.

So one evening at dusk, when I pass Alex's room and see him lying on his bed, reading, I feel less concerned than I might have. He looks adrift on his bed, or rather his bed looks adrift amid the darkening room, and he looks, sprawled out as he is, merely along for the ride.

The book Alex is reading is *They Cage the Animals at Night,* by Jennings Michael Burch. I read this book, a true story about a boy in foster care, and it was perhaps the saddest book I read. I liked it, I liked its depiction of old New York City, and the truth of the storyteller. Unlike many others, it feels inhabited, the story fully felt by the writer. But its sad mood is unremitting.

"Do you like it?" I say from the doorway.

"It's so sad. But it's good. But it's so sad."

I turn on his desk lamp, and then one in the room's corner. The gloom vanishes.

"When's Dad coming home?" he asks.

"Seven o'clock, as usual."

"Did you get the tickets?"

"I will."

"You will? You promise?" He sits up. "When? I mean how about now? They went on sale already. Nathan Lane is in it, Mom, you know he was in *Forum*. You think he's so funny. And Matthew Broderick—he was in *Ferris Bueller's Day Off*. That was his first movie. It's going to be so funny. I read all the early reviews. And Mel Brooks wrote the book, and the lyrics."

"OK," I say. "But it's too late now. I'll call tomorrow." I make up my mind quickly: this will be his present for his thirteenth birthday. We are not giving him a bar mitzvah, since we are not practicing Jews; this will be his gift. "What part are you up to in the book?"

"His mother left him," he says dully, sinking back down. "But he found his old friend from the orphanage again. At least he has that one friend. Does it get better? Nothing more bad happens, does it?"

I don't have the heart to tell him that the friend will die in a few pages, and so will everyone, except the little boy telling the story.

Later, Alex and Dan are playing music together. From

the vibrations of the walls, perhaps Clair is dancing. Alex is playing the piano, this after much prodding, since he has come to regard the piano as fraught with bad feelings, a stone around his neck; but he is playing nevertheless. He plays well, and secretly enjoys it, and he is accompanying Dan, who is playing the guitar. They sound good, although they keep breaking off and laughing. I make a note to myself to resume the search for a new teacher for Alex.

Alex has left his room ablaze with light, and I go in to turn off the lamps. *They Cage the Animals at Night* lies on the bed. I flip through the pages, the soft tuft fanning me. The sadness of the book returns. How does such a searing story about abandonment—this child's mother drops him off one day at an orphanage, with no explanation, and never is really able to retrieve him—how does such a story hit a twelve-year-old reader?

A friend of mine who is a psychiatrist in a city clinic told me that a twelve-year-old patient of hers, with a "train-wreck life"—foster care, abuse, horrible things—loved reading excessively traumatic books. "The girl eats them up," my friend said, "can't get enough. Finishes one, picks up another." This makes sense to me; I can imagine how reading about others in trouble could feel like a lifeline.

But how do the books hit a twelve-year-old or ten-year-old who still has a mother, whose life has all its parts more or less functioning, but who is just beginning the process of becoming more independent? What is the effect of hitting a kid with stories about abandonment and loss just at the moment that *he* is repositioning himself to separate?

The books evoke compassion, sure. They offer a glimpse

into other lives, broaden understanding of the inequities of society. Obviously this is good. But unless there is the assumption that children always remain slightly detached readers—sociological perspective foremost—don't stories with such potent, universal themes as abandonment and loss reverberate as personal stories?

Some of them must have been written as a kind of offering: to the child, to all children, who may at some point be in trouble. The book is a protector; the book reaches out. The child needs help.

I sit down on Alex's bed.

The troubling books are all squished together in his bookshelf. They have taken up residence. Seen as a group, they have a pushy, aggressive edge.

Just who is their intended reader? What assumptions have been made about that intended (ten- to twelve-year-old) reader?

Self-centered, unfeeling? Needs to be hit on the head repeatedly about how people suffer? Can't this approach inspire the opposite reaction—invite such a detached person to become even more detached? "A book must be an ice axe to break the sea frozen inside us," Kafka wrote. The child is frozen, the book's job is to hack away?

I pick up the book on Alex's bed again, and flip through it. This time a paper falls out of the tuft. It is a paragraph Alex must have typed, copied from *Newsweek*. It is from an article on foster care:

> The autopsy photo shows a little boy who looks relieved to be dead. His eyes are closed. A hospital tube protrudes through his broken nose. He has deep cuts above his right ear

> and dark linear scars on his forehead. The bruises on his back are a succession of yellows, greens, and blues. On the bottom of his tiny feet are third-degree burns. He had been battered and tortured.

On the bottom of the page, in clear print, Alex's teacher has written: "Excellent Choice Alex! A!"

This? A child relieved to be dead? In the whole wide world of literature, why is it imperative for twelve-year-olds to stare into the abyss of the abusive foster care system? Why? Why this of all things?

I stomp downstairs. Alex is eating a cookie in the kitchen. He looks cheerful. "I saw this article about foster care," I say casually, offering it. "It's an intense article. Why exactly did he have you read this?"

His face darkens. "It's for language arts. To go with *They Cage the Animals at Night.* We have to research the foster care system. Forget it. It's not important."

I don't know what to say. "But, it's so—Did you find it, I mean, what did you think of this article?"

"Please," he says. "Please. I don't want to talk about it!"

"But I just want to understand—"

"Leave me alone!"

I leave.

Chapter Seven

It is foggy on Tuesday, although in the morning light, golden leaves are visible; branches are black from rain.

"Don't be late," Clair says.

I promise her I won't be, and in truth I am eager to attend, to see her in her classroom, and hear her memoirs. Yet I have not shaken the sinking feeling with regard to the whole idea of this hired writing program; it seems, in some as yet indefinable way, of the same mind-set as problem novels, with their demand that children be in the world of only what is "real" and "inner." And the reality selected seems to exclude anything drawn from the imagination. What is the larger, overarching thinking about childhood that links together memoir for the young and problem novels?

During the week, I have been reading around in the books of Lucy Calkins, the head of the Writing Project, which runs out of Teachers College, Columbia University. This is the program that has trained and installed the expert in Clair's classroom. The Writing Project (now known as the Reading and Writing Project) is enormously popular and has found its way into schools all across America.

Calkins's prose sometimes swells with feeling, about her sincere desire to have children offered literature from the very start, for them to love writing, and for classrooms to have their own self-contained libraries and "Writing

Centers." All children, she maintains, should feel themselves to be "Readers" and "Writers" (she capitalizes these words), and she does not simply want mere mechanical skills. She wants reading to be an urgent, paramount desire for children, and for them to be "good" readers, a value that she spends much time distinguishing from "bad" readers.

Her books provide a wealth of information to teachers and parents on how to implement her ideas, and I can imagine that much of what she offers might be especially helpful to the novice teacher who is just setting up a classroom, or who is attempting to flood the classroom with literacy, with the love of books. She advocates reading aloud to children at every turn, even after they can read themselves. In her book *The Art of Teaching Writing,* for example, she offers nuts and bolts instructions on how to set up a Writing Center in the classroom, and also addresses the larger thinking behind her plans, as in the chapter "Writing Literature under the Influence of Literature." Much of her material is promising.

Yet when she strays into musing about parent-child relationships, as in her book *Raising Lifelong Learners,* written expressly for parents, or attempts, in general, to make explicit her philosophical underpinnings (which can feel unduly prescriptive), I am less impressed. In some of Calkins's particularly lofty riffs, there lurks a premise about childhood, memory in childhood, and the role of adults in the creative lives of children, that I find jarring.

Children, Lucy Calkins writes, need to be "woken up." They need to live "writerly" lives, which means to become "alerted to the poetry of their lives" and adept at recording such observations. They need adults to help them toward this goal. In fact, adults ought to be present at every turn to ensure this goal.

"For children to write better, they have to write often," she writes. "To ensure this happens, I try to make writing an everyday activity. . . . My sons each have a notebook, and are expected to write at least a page in their notebooks or elsewhere. . . . My advice (to parents) is *never miss a day*. If you allow kids to get off the hook once, they'll try to get off it all the time." One wonders what this heavy presence of mother in the creative realm feels like; it flies in the face of how so many writers have described the role of writing in their childhoods: secret, done under covers with a flashlight.

Children need to learn early how to revise their recordings, says Calkins. Such is the work of a "real writer." Even in kindergarten, Calkins believes, it is not too early to revise. A friend of mine who attended a workshop on this topic, sponsored by Calkins, described the presenter's suggestion that five-year-olds ought to be encouraged to do drafts of their artwork: Children ought to ask themselves, "How can I make my picture better?"

Calkins believes that she, and presumably other adults, can (and should) evaluate what is poetic in someone else's life. "My real goal . . . is for my sons to walk the trail of their whole lives, seeing small particulars which are worth lingering over. I help them to do this by *keeping my eyes and ears open for the potential poems and stories that are there in their lives*" (my emphasis).

Is it really possible to know what will be poetically meaningful to another person?

Teaching writing to her sons and grooming them toward "poetic observation" is apparently part of her family life. "I teach writing when my sons and I push aside the schoolwork on a winter's evening and go outside, to stand under the spell of the full moon," she writes. "'The moon makes the snow look . . . um . . . ,' I say. 'Glowing,' Evan answers, and his voice turns smooth, soft. In his best imitation of the poets he admires, he adds, 'glowing with a soft light.'"

Later she adds: "I let my children know that when they lag behind to peer closely at a little flower growing between the cracks in the sidewalk, they are living like poets. 'You are such observers!' I tell my boys. 'It's what gives you your writing talent!'"

The ostensible message here—that observation is key to a developing person's poetic sensibility, and that an observant adult, who shares his own observations, can be valuable—makes sense. Yet it is the *orchestration* of the poetic moment, as she describes it, that I find unsettling. It suggests that where the child assumed otherwise, the adult had an agenda; a certain dishonesty is implied. But more potentially destructive—at least to the developing poetic consciousness of a child, and unsettling inasmuch as this sensibility might be emulated in classrooms—is the extent to which the adult seems to have had the "poetry" of the evening already scripted.

Did Calkins have a certain word, or set of words in mind when she posed the unfinished sentence to her son? Was there a right and a wrong way to describe the moon?

The right approach to the moon (she may have conveyed, however wordlessly) was to speak of its beauty. The wrong way might have included references to, say, terror, or aggression.

The moon glows, the night is beautiful, but isn't it true also that the night can be rife with things lurking in shadows?

Elsewhere, in a section devoted to teaching parents how best to guide children toward polite behavior, Calkins reveals that she admonishes her sons when they offer a non sequitur in conversation. "The conversation will be on one thing, and they interject with a remark from left field. Invariably, we adults tend to think, Now where did that come from? but essentially overlook the detour. I don't think this is wise." She goes on to suggest that adults confront the child with his detour, and advise him instead to stick to the topic at hand. (Doesn't so much of poetry come from the sudden swerve of non sequiturs?) This advice strikes me as an indication that profound, if mannerly, thought-control might be at work. And if this is operative, it needs to be asked: How free are children in this Calkins universe to express what they might truly feel? Is there a spoken, or unspoken, agenda about what kind of material is acceptable and what is not? Doesn't so much of feeling, poetic and otherwise, come from left field? The invitation to poetic reflection is genuinely meaningful only when any and all demons, too, are welcome to leap on the page.

With regard to the content of children's writing: Not only is Calkins's mission to get kids to continually record, become transcribers (and revisionists) of their experiences, but she has a decided view on what kinds of things children should record. She writes about herself in classrooms:

> As I move about the room, I pull my chair alongside one child after another in order to listen intently. . . . When we respond to young writers in these ways, we are teaching important lessons. Our children's lives brim full of concerns and stories, and yet when we ask them to write about their experiences they often say, "Nothing happens in my life." When we suggest they choose their own topics for writing, they often write about superheroes or re-tell television drama. In word and deed, our children ask, Does my life really matter?

Toward this end she makes the mainstay of her program the writing of nonfiction only: this in memoir, personal essays, and daily journal entries. Writing about real life, presumably, draws children into realizing how important their lives are. In this regard, her approach to children's experience is similar to that of many of the problem novels I read: above all, the narrative needs to stick to the actual.

Does the requirement to write only "what really happened" and exclusively about oneself, feel liberating?

I began wondering these things as a result of the complaint of an eight-year-old boy who was in a classroom where Calkins's writing curriculum was under way. The boy's sibling, incidentally, has a fatal disease, and the boy is thus living with the specter of death on a daily basis; perhaps he could have used the opportunity of a Writer's Notebook as a place for catharsis. Yet he hated the whole megillah. He found writing in school impossible, and had to be forced to write, his teacher sitting over him, a whole stubborn dynamic in place. He was furious, he told me later, not that he had to write—in fact he wrote copiously at home and wanted to grow up to be a writer—but that he couldn't really write how he wanted. "We can't make up any stories," he marveled. "We can't write about death. No one can die." Presumably had he chosen to write in direct, nonfiction prose ("My sister has a disease. I am worried . . ."), this would have been accepted, even welcomed, by any well-meaning teacher. In fact, I believe this is the kind of revelation valued by teachers in the Writing Project. But this was clearly not how this boy, at this time in his life, desired to tell his story. Another of his complaints about the tyranny of the Writer's Notebook indicated to me the way he *did* wish to write about life: "I want to write about haunted houses," he said.

And why can't children write fiction in Calkins's program? She has said that this is because children are not sophisticated enough to write fiction. But I think that she believes that writing what "really happened" is, somehow, healthy. Is there a suspicion of the unconscious? The unexamined? What might slip out if not monitored? What about the truth that is told in symbolic language?

For that matter, is it in a child's nature to want to reflect on himself? Or reflect too much in general? Or to "cherish" his memories, as an adult might? Children, unlike adults, do not spend their time talking directly about themselves. In play dates, for example, their chatter is not, as it is for adults, or even for adolescents, a succession of topics having to do with how one felt, or what one did, or the ins and outs of one's inner experience: in play dates, at least the ones I've been privy to, kids do stuff, make stuff, roam around, and seek out the world. The self is in motion; the self is synonymous with being and doing, and is implicit; but the impulse to hoist up the "I" as the overarching, self-conscious topic is not apparent. In short, aren't children and adults fundamentally different? Or so I imagine asking Calkins.

Perhaps Calkins would argue that for children, when an adult asks, both actually and implicitly, "Well, what about You? I'm interested in Your life, not TV characters," this can have a transformative effect. I do not doubt this. This kind of respect paid to a child's life and observations tells the child that his experience matters, and that an adult is interested. And certainly to tack down experience in writing can offer that experience up for reflection and "ownership." My point is rather this: Interest in a child's experience, as a means toward vitalizing writing is constraining, not expanding, if I insist that the only meaningful story a child can relay is one that is actual. By the same token, insisting that a child is having a thoughtful, poetic, observant existence only when he is recording in his notebooks, is to misunderstand, and greatly underestimate, the role of incubation in creative thought. Daydreaming and fantasy in childhood can be so rich and satisfying as to not need, and even actually resist, outward documentation—at any rate just yet.

I recall Clair and three friends over after school recently, two boys and a girl, and how they plowed into her dress-up box, and came out wearing wigs and huge sunglasses, and talked in accents. (They tell me they have made up a play called *London's Deepest*.) They tend to stay in character. In dressing up, are they suggesting that their real selves are not important? Are they hiding from reality? One could argue that they are in fact exploring reality, and in the "free-est" and fullest way possible. Can't writing about superheroes be tantamount to dressing-up in play? What if your real self—who, after all, is under continual transformation and subject to rediscovery throughout childhood—is best expressed in games of pretend?

On this last point, I ponder a story that a parent of a first grader told me. Her son, also under the tutelage of an expert from the Writing Project, was asked to write his first "piece" and wrote about two lizards who were brothers, who flew to the sun, and their tails caught on fire. To me this story sounded very promising, an economical story, in the way that a story in a dream is condensed yet deeply expressive. The response by the expert, however, was that the boy needed to "seriously re-think his material," and rewrite it, this time writing about his "real" brother and the things they "really" did together.

The boy had written the lizard story with verve and delight, declaring he loved writing. Upon hearing that his story was unacceptable, and that he now had to rewrite it, this time about real life, he became very upset, because, he told his mother, he had already written about his brother—presumably in the way he wanted to, as a fellow lizard in a great adventure. He did not want to write about his actual brother; that, he said, was too boring. But the expert insisted. After this he claimed to hate writing.

I found the report of this interchange disturbing. I wanted to ask the Writing Project expert: What if a child loves animals, and they take important lead roles in stories, in part because animals, in their silence, express all that one feels, but can't express directly?

Such, anyway, were the sorts of thoughts I was having as I made my way, excited, curious, yet tense, to Clair's Memoir Reading.

Alfred Kazin has written that his elementary school was "like a factory over which has been imposed the façade of a castle." This conjures for me the exact imperial creepiness of my own elementary school—its wire fences, dreary halls, metal doors, yet fluted pillars flanking the metal doors.

In contrast, Clair's school is a low, U-shaped building, surrounded by beautiful red maples, and even though the fog is thick, the lights shining from within the large windows that flank the front of the building make the school cheery. Orange paper pumpkins dot the glass. Up close, I can see directly into kindergarten rooms, where small children are happily playing. A teacher waves.

I always feel excited to enter the school. It is friendly here, but more than that, my children have had good teachers and good experiences, and each feels positive about school as a result. As I walk to Clair's classroom, I pass a straggling line of small children filing through the hall en route to somewhere, and they are headed by a teacher Alex had back when he was in first grade. Her charges seem relaxed, even dreamy, evidencing none of the strict handling that we, as young children, endured. These straggly kids, passing in their languid style, with their cheerful teacher more or less leading them onward, bring to mind the phrase "herding cats."

Clair's classroom is bustling. We spot each other immediately and wave. There is a table laden with brownies, brightened by haphazard M&M's, meant obviously for a big turnout of parents. And indeed there are many of us; in fact each child seems to have at least one adult in attendance. Many of us adults know each other, and a good feeling prevails. We chat, and stroll along the perimeter of the room, admiring children's artwork, much of which is of falling leaves, and squirrels gathering acorns, of bears who have curled in caves for the winter. "Did parents come into our classrooms—ever—when we were kids?" I ask a friend, who shakes her head no, and adds, "I don't remember them coming even once." We marvel, then, how all of us are here, how times have changed, how we, unlike our parents, have been invited into our children's classroom. Why were our parents barred? What would it have been like to have had my parents come? For a moment I picture them walking down those quiet halls, their bearing tentative, nearly cowed, as if they were foreigners—which might have been how they felt, that is, as Jews in a school run by Irish teachers, in a school that strove above all to be American, which meant no whiff of any other culture, not even the culture of home.

But here we are, we parents, chatting away, even dipping into the pile of brownies, which the teacher (a gifted, poetic woman, whom Alex still recalls as his favorite) admonishes us politely, "are meant for after the reading." We laugh, and apologize, and make jokes how we are like little kids and need to be reminded to control our appetites. The teacher asks us to please come now and sit, that the reading is about to begin. At this point, Clair runs to me and hugs me, and whispers, "My ear hurts again." I feel her forehead, but she has no fever, and in fact looks radiantly healthy, as usual. I say, "Does it hurt so much that you want to go home now? Or can you stick it out?" She says, "I can stick it out."

The parents sit on little chairs, which have been arranged around the children, who now have assembled on the rug. The children seem smaller than I remember them being in "real life"; they are fresh-faced, obedient, each with an oversized, laminated book entitled *My Life* resting on their small knees. I look around for the expert, and take it that she is not here, but that this "celebration" is a product of her work. Clair is sitting up straight, in exaggerated good posture, a suggestion that she is being ultracooperative, and even though I know we will go to the doctor soon enough, I am heartened by her rosy cheeks, her apparent fine heath. From this detached distance, I note the line of her forehead in profile, and something about the wide spacing of her eyes and the shape of her face looks remarkably familiar, not only as herself, but as myself as a child, and I have a sudden clear sense, not for the first time, that I am seeing at last what I looked like back then, when I was a child.

One at a time, children begin reading from their books.

After each, we enthusiastically applaud. "My mother always cooked me vanilla pudding," one little boy reads. "She got out all the lumps." He keeps stealing glances at his mother, a woman I know well; she is smiling, and blushing, although from the way she is holding her head back in a tilt, I can tell she is trying to keep tears contained.

In fact, I feel like crying too. Why? Have we been stirred by how much we love our children, how vulnerable they are? Are we remembering our own childhoods? Why is this so moving, hearing our children reminisce about their own childhoods?

I am confused by all this unexpected feeling, and as I swallow to keep down my tears, for a moment I feel oversized in this small seat—which of course I am, but it is more of a surreal feeling, as if the chair is far, far too small, the size of a cup, and I am an adult-sized child, teetering on the rim. I am relieved to see that no one at all is looking at me, and this fact allows me to shrink back down a bit to my actual outlines. By the stillness of everyone, the hyperarched attentiveness, and the balled-up Kleenexes, I see that I am not the only one trying to contain whatever strange emotions are being stirred.

"My father put me to bed every night," another boy reads. "But first we would wrestle. He put his feet up and I would ride my stomach on his feet like I was an airplane. I always pretended I was flying." The child is adorable, small, with red ears and a neat little buttoned-down shirt that looks a bit old-fashioned to me. We applaud, and he bows.

And I think, this is amazing, truly amazing, that a child sits in a public school classroom, and shares such an intimate experience as a bedtime ritual with his father. A huge cultural shift indeed. I try to picture us, my little second-grade class back in 1964, sitting around on the floor (the floor!) reading to each other about ourselves in our homes, about how we acted when we got ready for sleep. Unthinkable, totally unthinkable, nearly as inappropriate as coming to school in your pajamas—which, I recall, Alex's whole class did back in kindergarten, on Pajama Day. In fact, we hid the fact of our personal lives, just as we would never have dreamed of bringing in any food made at home.

And it is all of a piece, I think, the relaying of personal stories and the presence of parents in the school, a piece of the same cultural trend. The home is being invited into school, the private, with all its "diversity," brought into the public, and this celebration of the personal expresses itself through the love of the first-person narrator. The "I" prevails. When *I* was young, nothing I came across in school was written in the First Person; no one poked out from beneath the majestic omniscient narrator.

The memoirs continue, and I am succeeding, more or less, in retaining my composure. But the undercurrent of sadness continues too, even during the happy memoirs about picnics and parties; the sadness seems both to detract from and heighten the charm of the children's writing, by making their memoirs, somehow, more poignant. Again I feel the slightly surreal sense of being too large, of the chair being far, far below me. After a while, I look away, toward the wall of windows in the back, beyond the children's small heads. Dark branches are barely visible through thick fog. A bird swoops by.

I do not remember being able to look out of the window when I was in school in New York City, years ago; the shades were always drawn. I remember blanked-out windows. I remember the shades as flesh-colored, wholly opaque. "The outside," our teachers explained, "is too distracting."

It is Clair's turn to read from her memoir. "My mother would hug me, and I would snuggle in her soft arms." I watch her while she reads, her shiny wild hair, today subdued with red barrettes, her dimples, her expressive eyes. She has written about us. Her voice is very clear. "My mother would hold me when my ear hurt, and I would feel safe in her arms." For a moment I am flushed with too much feeling, with love and embarrassment and pride, and worry about her ear, all at once, and, like all the mothers whose children have already read, I am crying freely now. But while I cry, and beam with pride, I am uneasy. Why?

When she closes her book, and bows, and sits back down, I suddenly know. It is that this memoir reading feels a bit like a eulogy. We have all been cast in the strange light of the dead. In the quirky conditional voice with which Clair has written about our lives as if all the things in our lives are over, have already passed, used to be, "would" occur, and are present now only as memory, the implication is that these things occur no more. We have all been forced to imagine a time when this moment we are sharing together has vanished.

And this is not a natural way that children see. One must have traveled to the end of something to be able to have a satisfying backward perspective. This whole enterprise is something adults have imposed. And why? Why is my generation hell-bent on making our children wake from the dream of their childhoods? So they can fast-forward to a time when their childhoods are over, safely encoded in memory? So they are like adults, dreamy with nostalgia?

I am thinking of bears as the last round of applause dies down, and the children take a group bow, and everyone is wiping tears. I am imagining creeping into a cave to shake a bear awake: it is difficult, and he is logy, but he stirs. "Why not let him wake when he's ready?" I think of screaming. "Why not believe his sleep is necessary and good?"

We eat brownies, and Clair makes sure I get one she designed, entirely with yellow M&M's. The parents congratulate the children on their wonderful memoirs. Clair tells me her ear doesn't hurt at all anymore, and I hug her goodbye. It is late morning when I leave, I am a bit discombobulated, and the air is dense with fog, so dense that it appears to be snowing, although it is not. I am walking across a vast ball field. It is only possible to see things in the immediate foreground, a sudden black tree, and then my shoes, and if I hold them up, my hands. I'm glad I walked here, and do not have to drive home.

I am sunk in thought as I walk. I feel that same sad, strange feeling as in the classroom, but out here, nearly invisible, I am able to separate from it all, think everything over. I try to hear my footsteps to orient myself. Once or twice I notice a blackbird walking through the fog. He does not seem to notice me, although his head, like a spool of black thread, keeps poking through the fog near me.

Is there a cost to thrusting a young child into the spotlight? Can he become lit up for others to see, but blinded to himself?

I am sunk in my thoughts, although aware of the proximity of the black head in the fog next to me, the shiny eye looking all the time straight ahead. I stop for a moment, and I hear the bird rustling, which gratifies me for some reason, and then he stops. We are both standing here in this fog, neither of us with any shadow, and it feels as if we are not standing, but bobbing, as if we are drifting in idle foam.

Hello, I think. But he is not accessible, not like a dog. For an instant in the shifting fog, I catch that his feathers have the black iridescence of charcoal, that he is fat, and is fully occupying his outlines. His eye is regarding me. Why does he stay so near but not look at me directly? Is he spooked by this fog?

And on and on, we are bobbing and I am thinking of the sea, that we are in a white vast foam of sea, and of what it might be like to be a bird, and I remember a line of a poem a child wrote once: "I am a woman with the mind of a rabbit," it began. I have always loved that line. Through the fog glows a streetlamp, whose light only serves to illuminate a cup of moving fog.

But then I imagine Lucy Calkins calling to me. "Write about this! This is huge! You are a writer!" and then "You are such an observer!" Immediately, suddenly, I am aware that life is motion, since it has instantly, if only for a moment, come to a crashing halt. I am shy with myself, and look around to see if anyone else is near, but of course I can't see if they are. The bird seems flatter now, like the birds we used to cut out of construction paper in school.

Where was I? I try to re-enter the earlier, dreamier state, but something has shifted: now I am only with myself out here, and instead of me and a blackbird, in foam, I am watching myself from a great distance, watching myself as I watch the bird, watching myself try to think up words to capture him: "black," "unusual" come to mind, but no other words follow. I try to remember how he looked before I tried to see him, but it is as if he is gone, and only this flat bird remains.

The next day I tiptoe into Clair's classroom, so I can pick her up for a doctor's appointment. The blackbirds are everywhere outside her window.

The children are seated again on the rug, but it is not Clair's teacher in front, but a stranger, a heavy woman, dressed in black and very serious, whom I know right away to be the expert. So intently is she speaking to the children, that she doesn't look up when I come in, although I sense that if she knew I was here, she would not like it, that this is closed to the public, especially to parents. I sit very still.

She is speaking in a monotone, and at first from the seriousness of the voice, and the sober expressions of the children, I think she is admonishing them for something they've done before I entered. But this is a very well-behaved class, and when I listen more closely I realize she is talking about poetry, about "living a writerly life." I look at Clair, who doesn't see me, and is listening intently, although it seems with an edge of nervousness. The expert is giving them very precise instructions on how to outline the stories in their lives, only some of which I can hear. She is holding up yellow Post-it notes, and everyone is quiet. "Jot down all ideas you have on these yellow Post-its. Otherwise you won't remember."

Behind her is that large window that faces the woods. As she stands pointedly holding the Post-its, her back to the glass, what looks like hundreds of blackbirds are flapping urgently, filling up the bare branches in a huge tree. If this were an illustration, it would have been done as splots of black ink. The children see; how could they not? They are calling out, "Look! Look!" But she refuses to turn around, and instead has crossed her arms, is saying patiently, "Excuse me. Haven't I asked you to keep the focus on poetry?"

The children shrug and giggle, and look around at each other. But they are a compliant group, quiet, and besides, they can watch the birds at the same time as seeming to watch her. There really is a huge number of birds, and they have gathered all on one tree, as if for some meeting. The branches bend from their collective, black weight; hundreds of orange leaves are showering from the tree. This is all silent to us, but must be a true commotion outside. The blackbirds seem agitated, in serious dispute. This is a huge event in the woods. Still she doesn't turn around, and has now resumed talking. "Always plan ahead!" she is saying.

Isn't this a perfect "teachable moment"—a poetical intrusion that could be written about? "Turn around!" I silently call to her, and wiggle in my seat so that she might notice me, and get my message. But she does not notice.

And just as suddenly as they appeared, the birds are now departing, as if they have arrived at a frenzied conclusion and can't waste another second. The branches spring up as they take off. The expert continues to steadfastly look ahead, waiting for full attention, which the children are doing their best to feign. I stop moving, and am glad she hasn't seen me. It's better this way, I realize, that nothing has been remarked upon. It's exhilarating to see the birds ascend behind her back.

Chapter Eight

I wish someone would tell me what to do.

Clair has run on ahead. She knows nothing of what will have to happen now. I imagine she has turned the TV on, and is under a blanket. The wind is fierce around the house. The windows of the porch fly open and shut from the wind.

In my coat pocket are bunched-up pages the doctor handed me, explaining Clair's condition, the nature of the surgery she must suddenly have, and several pages of risk factors. He had looked in her ear, and said, "I see a shadow in there"; I was still making chitchat, even though Clair was uncomfortable with the way he was pulling her ear, and yet he kept looking in. We were sent for a CAT scan, but still I didn't expect that there would be anything bad. Just another ear infection. But the doctor, holding the CAT scan to the light, said, "This is not good."

As I enter the porch, a window flies wide open, just one, and in from the black rectangle of night the wind rouses a pile of newspapers, levitating them almost to the ceiling, and they cling to each other up there, like a frail dance the dead might do, if given one last chance. Then the window slams shut again. The newspapers drift down.

My house is a succession of tiny rooms that make you switch left, then right, then left. My house, as they say, has no "flow." Someday we will knock these walls down and transform everything.

I pass Alex in an inner room, bent over a book, doing his homework. We wave, exactly as if we were on a train. I have taken my coat with me all this way; I lay it on the table, back here at the end of the house. I take out a cucumber and begin scraping it. With each scrape, I exhale. I cut a carrot, and put the carrot and cucumber together in a blue bowl. I am starting to feel better. The blue bowl, with the bright carrot and the green cucumber heaped in its core, seems familiar, friendly. Ever since we left the doctor's office everything has felt crammed up into one breathless crowd of urgent matters. The world has felt far away, but also too close up. Now, the blue bowl is comforting, and I am breathing normally.

❧ ❧ ❧

"Why are you sitting in the dark?" Dan's voice startles me. He is a tall man, dark, forthright. He fills up the kitchen doorway. Gently, as he turns on the light, he adds, "Tell me exactly what the doctor said."

"She needs surgery. She has a tumor, but it's benign. It's in her middle ear. That's why her ear infections never totally cleared up." I speak as if I were steeped in the whole thing, a weary mother who has already filled out pages of release forms, and is on top of everything, and is merely informing him. Actually it is his silence that forces me to hear my words.

"These tumors almost always grow back. They are very hard to get rid of. And the only way you can see if the previous surgery was successful is to do another surgery. CAT scans can't pick them up the second time. We're looking at at least two surgeries, but quite possibly more." (Much later, when all was over, I heard of someone who had had twenty-one surgeries for this condition, because the tumor kept growing back.) I tell him about the audiologist, about Clair's hearing loss. There are aspects of the surgery we do not discuss, not just yet.

He is quiet but then asks, "What's the risk if there's no operation?" I had asked this too, and the doctor, a young man who had been almost breezy up to this point, and who I had imagined would say, "Well of course there's always the option to do nothing," had suddenly looked up over the X-ray and said flatly, "You have no choice. This thing has a life of its own."

"No choice," I say.

Clair is in the doorway now. She has changed into her nightgown, which is red, and I can't quite tell if she has overheard us, although I imagine in some way she has. But all she says is, "I'm starving! What's for dinner?"

"Spaghetti and salad." I tip the blue bowl up as if to reassure her. She nods and leaves. I make dinner.

Dan and I are jittery, beginning sentences, exiting rooms abruptly, and picking up sometime later as if no time has passed. Alex is reading a book called *Ransom,* and out of habit I call out to him, as I walk by, "What's this one about?"

"Kids and their bus driver get kidnapped, and they're being held for ransom."

"Oh," I say. "That's nice."

Somehow we eat. Alex and Clair go to bed.

Later, up in our bedroom, Dan shows me printouts from the Internet, information about Clair's condition. Although it is a rare condition, there is a Web site devoted to it. We study the photographs, our bed and floor covered over with pictures of the canals of the middle ear, which are unimaginably narrow and labyrinthine. We discuss the whole thing over and over, repeating some of the stranger aspects we are finding out about, and then fall silent. We punctuate all the information with silence, while we absorb what is now unfolding. Our talking, followed by silence, reminds me of a machine that first states things in English and then goes silent while it plays the same message across the world in foreign languages.

Dan has spoken to an anesthesiologist we know, who reassures us about safety on the operating table. Dan continues making calls. He speaks with our pediatrician, who says she has never come across this condition in any children in her practice. This is not reassuring.

I watch my husband on the phone. His dark eyes are glittering; he is writing down information. I rest my head on his shoulder, and feel his muscles moving as he writes. I stay like that. Pictures of the middle ear continue to spew from our printer.

Sometime after midnight, Dan and I fall asleep, exhausted. But almost immediately, it seems, I wake with a start. The feeling of safety, which has always lulled our days, seems to have slipped away.

Staring up at the slanted ceiling, I recall the feeling in so many kids' books I've been thinking about: life bangs you around; you have to cope. I need to help Clair cope. I need to lead the way. Those books are all about survival; maybe I've been too dismissive of them. What might help? But I am too tired to think clearly. I can't settle on any one idea. I conjure just a feeling: thudding. I've landed with a thud.

I need to relax. How? I am too tired to read, but too jittery to sleep.

The window is shaking in the wind, and a branch scrapes against the glass. In the wind, all night, I hear warnings. I sit up, I lie down, I walk. I get back in bed.

After a while, I begin to tell myself a story, as I used to long ago when I was young and couldn't sleep. "Once there was a white house," and as soon as I begin to form these words, I am pulling something white across my mind, like the smoothness of a page. It is the binding comfort of a story.

I envision clearly each picket of our fence, each picket sunk deep in the earth. The fence encircles the house, encloses it, and I whisper in my mind, "Once upon a time there was a white house and a fence . . ." and in the aura of sleepiness, the fence and house grow softer, taking on the smoothness of sea glass. It is snug within. After a while the house, and the white fence, and the soft yard, are made of snow, and the snow is lit by a candle, hastily stuck in by a squirrel. As the pale, glowing scene melts in tone, I slide to sleep.

We have scheduled a date for the surgery, which is three weeks from now. How can I prepare Clair emotionally for her operation? She ought to be able to feel like an active participant, this much I know. To have some sense of power, as opposed to feeling merely acted upon. This goes for me too, for all of us.

Her doctor gives us the phone number of a mother whose child underwent the same operation Clair will have, and I call her. The conversation proves haunting, a cautionary tale:

"I didn't tell her much beforehand," the mother says. "Just the day of the surgery, I said, 'We're going to the doctor, to get a little procedure.'"

"Did she know what 'procedure' meant?"

"No, that's why I used it. She went off like a trooper."

"Oh."

"So that one went OK. They tell you it will be about three hours, but it was more like five, even six. It's a long time under general anesthesia, but just so you know, it takes longer than they say. And they have to have at least two surgeries, you know. So the first one was OK. The hospital stay, the whole thing, was OK. But. Going back to the operating room the second time was much worse. For the second one we did the same, didn't say anything until we got to the hospital, didn't really mention even the word 'procedure,' but this time as soon as she got to the hospital she became hysterical, and they had to sedate her. I mean completely hysterical."

The woman has been matter-of-fact in her telling, brisk, someone whom I could imagine in another context saying "Get over it already." But now she is saying something else, but because she is crying, I can't make out the words.

"She hasn't spoken since," she manages to say. "She won't talk. She's become a mute."

Clair and Dan and I meet with the Child Life Services, a program in the hospital that helps children and families emotionally prepare for surgery. Alex comes too. The purpose is to inform, because the more you know beforehand and the more you know what to expect, the less trauma is likely. The hospital is vast and bustling, but up on the floor where we meet, it is quiet and seems orderly enough. I am nervous, so nervous that my mouth seems always dry, but I feel better for the first time in days, now that we are actually doing something. I want to be helpful and brave for Clair.

We are met by a young woman, a calm, attentive person, who shows us a videotape called "My Operation," narrated by children. Dan and Alex and I sit upright and view it carefully, although Clair doesn't watch it, but sits at a nearby table and puts together a puzzle. I gather she is sort of listening. Later she remarks that it was "boring," which Alex agrees with, and they both think it would have gone better if Mel Brooks had narrated it. We are trying to keep our spirits lively. The woman returns, and gives us a tour of the places we will encounter on the day of the surgery, and afterward: the waiting room, the pre-op room, where she presents us with the strange blue outfits Dan and I will have to wear, including hair and shoe coverings, so that we can accompany Clair to the operating room. We begin to put them on, for sort of a dress rehearsal, but Clair says she "isn't in the mood." We see the operating room through a small glass window, and Clair stands on her tiptoes and peers inside. This is the first moment she is giving her full attention. "Do they make pizza in there?" she asks. We laugh, but I don't know exactly what to say.

She gets a bit kooky. The woman gives Clair things to handle: stethoscope, IV tubes, oxygen and anesthesia mask. Clair is given a teddy bear to tend to, as if he is the patient and she the doctor, and she jerks the bear around aggressively—the worst doctor in the world—shoving the stethoscope in his mouth, squishing his ears. Alex is polite and observant, and other than Clair's banter, the sterile room is totally quiet. We are not used to seeing Clair this revved up, giddy. It is interesting. I am a little embarrassed in front of this sedate young woman, who is standing with her hands behind her back, nodding. I want to explain, "She's not usually like this," but I don't.

That night Clair is still giddy, zooming around, eyes glittering, although now it is easier to detect the force of anxiety behind her zooming. We eat, and talk, and she lies near me to rest. I unpack a box of books that were given to me by my elderly aunt, who has since died, and who had been a social worker for the poor. The box is full of old and interesting books. I pull out a book of photojournalism called *You Have Seen Their Faces,* by Erskine Caldwell and Margaret Bourke-White. It was published in 1937 by Union Labor, which I take to be part of the WPA. I have never seen this book before, although I sense it must have been a radical book in its day, and as I look through it, I see that it retains its power. It is a collection of clear black-and-white photos: of sharecroppers, of "Negro" children, of the rural South. "The legends under the pictures are intended to express the authors' own conceptions of the sentiments of the individuals portrayed; they do not pretend to reproduce the actual sentiments of these persons," reads the disclaimer at the front of the book.

I turn the pages slowly. The pictures are stark. Many are of children—young, subdued looking, obviously tamed by the presence of the camera; they are sitting on tattered beds, or swallowed by tobacco fields. All barefoot, all bony and thin. But it is their faces that achieve arresting significance: calm, nearly dreaming faces, but eyes expressive with feeling—curiosity, kindness, hopelessness. The children in the photographs are not victims, or if they are, they are not portrayed as seeing themselves as victims. The photos do not beg the reader for pity, so much as invite the reader to stop and consider the individual lives on the pages. A boy, who looks to be around seven, stands in a doorway of a shack with a wonderful-looking hound; both look tentative and shy, but by how close they stand to each other, it's obvious they are great companions. "Blackie ain't good for nothing, he's just an old hound dog," the caption reads.

I call Clair over to look too, and she settles closer to me. "Look at this beautiful book I found," I say. "Do you want to see these children?" I try to explain the context for the photographs, the racist South, the lives of the poor. Lying near me, she carefully studies each picture of children. Two skinny cute children in rags, about her age, seven, stand in what looks like a shack, wallpapered with newspapers. I await her comments, and after a while she says, "Are they alone? Where are the parents?"

I study the picture. "Oh I'm sure their parents are somewhere. Anyway," I hasten to add, "what else do you notice about their house?" I want her to see that it is covered with newspaper, that the children are poor. I keep trying to edge her toward the larger sociological tale that these photographers were after, and brush her question aside. "But are you sure they're inside?" she keeps repeating, and peers so close to the page that her nose touches it, as if by being this close she might be able to detect them.

"Of course I'm sure," I say, and add, "But look at the poor shack they live in. Their walls are covered in newspaper to keep them warm. They have no heat."

But she is sitting up now, and her voice is loud. "How do you know their parents are inside? How do you know?"

I am growing a little annoyed. These are irrelevant questions. "Forget the parents," I want to say. But then I realize the questions are not irrelevant to her. At age seven, this is all that matters: that parents are near.

⁂

Clair and I stay together a lot before the operation. We go for walks, and chat, holding hands. With regard to the surgery, I feel that I try to run ahead of her and gather information, and then tell her things in small narratives, so that she can be prepared, know what to expect. I hear more about risk factors, the fate of her hearing, but of course I say nothing to her of any of this. I try to keep my tone bright. "When we go to the hospital," I say, "I'll stay with you the whole time." She likes this, and smiles a little. "Who will take care of Alex?" she asks, worrying for him, but relishing, I think, this time alone with me. I tell her Daddy will, and Granny will come too.

On Saturday Clair comes with me to do errands, and at the last minute we decide to walk to town, rather than take the car. It is only on the way back—me lugging dry cleaning, she a sack of oranges—that the sky darkens, and it seems like this was a bad idea. We hear thunder. Suddenly the October wind is cold, and wet leaves are flying everywhere.

The church, the one where we hold Story Shop, is just up ahead, and we decide to duck inside. As usual, the heavy front door is unlocked, the stone entry is welcoming in its quiet way, but it is clear that not a soul is here. The wind bangs on the old roof.

Usually I find the emptiness of the church comfortable, but today I wish there were someone else here. Some solid adult to exchange pleasantries with: "Raining yet?" "Not quite." I try to dispel the gloom in the stone hall by turning on the overhead light, but as usual it is weak. Thunder reverberates loudly through the silence. "I'm scared," Clair whispers. "I'll call Dad to pick us up," I say, my voice normal.

But when I turn into the office to use the phone, my heart is pounding. Out of the window, the rising wind and the heavy, fast-shifting clouds look like the open sea; I have a fleeting image of drowning. In over my head, out of my depth. How can I be so worked up over a simple storm? My uneasiness continues to rise, bordering on panic, even though I recognize that it is all out of proportion, that the pending storm—the wind is flinging a garbage can down into the street, so it rolls into traffic—must be expressing all that I am trying not to feel: the world is unpredictable and violent; loss is possible.

I sit down, and focus on the tidy desk blotter. A small, even, square of green. No one has even doodled on it. I run my hands over the felt expanse, and trace its edges. "Be Here Now," I whisper to myself. "Stay In The Moment. One Day At A Time. Know What You Can't Control." The slogans have only a slight calming effect. I take a deep breath. But then Clair is shouting, "Mommy! Come quick!" and even to myself my hectic motions—I get up so fast I knock over my chair—are overly dramatic. We nearly collide in the hall. She grabs my hand and we race to the Green Room. "Look!" she says, jumping.

The room, half sunk in darkness, half suffused with this weird green light, is like an aquarium. The thing she is pointing to is in the greeny half: a small bureau I remember buying at a tag sale for fifty cents long ago—junky, but now lit up, like someone plain revealed suddenly to be beautiful. The light drenches the whole structure—the size of Clair herself—the otherwise battered wood, and six, small, warped drawers ignited now to a brilliant shine.

On top of the bureau rests a large boot box, and deep inside is a peaceful, green atmosphere. On white sand, undisturbed, are tangled, real-looking dark leaves. On one cardboard wall is a rippling shadow, like the reflections of a pool. What causes it? I poke my finger under a leaf, and see an orb of glass. (I recognize that orb! It was a stopper that used to fit perfectly into an old perfume bottle. The bottle has been lost for years.) The light hitting the glass casts wobbly prisms on the otherwise calm cardboard wall.

"It's Lizard Motel!" Clair declares. My heart is still beating fast, and it takes me a moment to realize that her tone is triumphant, no longer spooked, as if we'd been hiking for hours and at last have come upon this hidden motel. "Dexter made it."

"Lizard Motel," I repeat, matching her triumphant tone. I regard the brilliant bureau. The project had been made a year ago, played with, finished, never taken home. Left in the corner. But here it's been, in these rainy shadows. It's been here, thriving all along.

We peer more deeply in the box: A turquoise toy lizard (the motel proprietor) propped upside down against one cardboard wall, nose to the ground, pausing as he is about to step one tiny foot (toenails so precise) onto the flooring of white sand. He has a slight tilt to his small head, and appears to be staring straight back at us. Something about the tilt of the lizard's head, and his defiance of gravity—how has he stayed just where he was propped a year before? —conjures Dexter himself: a small boy with perfectly upright posture, neat, deliberate, even when he tilted to pour the sand out of his knapsack; his shiny, perfectly straight black hair fanned out sideways, but when he was done pouring, his hair snapped right back into place, as it always does. A gallant, neat boy. Green madras shirt, never wrinkled.

"Let's see the rooms," Clair whispers. She slides open the first drawer—"The Poison Room," Dexter had told us, where the lizards "keep poison." A second turquoise lizard peers defiantly back at us from in here, knee-deep in shriveled berries and saffron threads. Then "The Weapon Room," whose drawer contains an evil-looking corkscrew, and here too is another lizard, peering slyly up at us. I remember Dexter sliding these drawers open, a good boy smelling of soap, but also gleaming with this dangerous power.

Then Clair pulls open "The Jewel Room," which is entirely filled with glitter. It still spangles. A lizard resides in here, a dark red lizard. "The butler," Dexter had said. Clair closes each drawer carefully. She briefly checks the remaining drawers, which are empty—as they should be, since these are the rooms left for guests.

"Look in the back of the last room," I whisper, because I remember something.

Sure enough, tucked in the last drawer, folded up into a piece no bigger than a tooth, is a paper. She unfolds it, which takes a while, and while she does the unfolding, I regard her, her little fingers, her beautiful face, fully engrossed. Lizard Motel is making us feel better. Why? I notice a few leaves caught in the back of her hair. Her hair is wild—she hates to brush it. We fight about this sometimes. Sometimes she hides the brush.

I realize I have relaxed, even though the thunder continues. For the moment, though, in the light of the jungle, the weather makes sense.

When she hands me the paper, I take it with a feeling of anticipation: I had liked something about the odd sense of time in his story. What was it?

In his neat, vertical pencil print, as I read aloud, we hear

Dexter enunciating each word, resting his white teeth, probably still baby teeth, on edge to pause at the end of each sentence.

> Lizard Motel
>
> The Lizard is Gone. Chapter one.
>
> One day the butler came up to the lizard's room, but there is no one there. He looks everywhere, but the lizard isn't anywhere. So he gave up.

Clair picks up a lizard from the jewel drawer and enacts the search, imitating how she saw Dexter animate him while he read his story aloud.

> Lots of people started coming to the motel.
>
> But there are only three spaces left for guests.
>
> The lizard has been gone for two weeks now. Some of the guests have left, and some new ones have come.
>
> It's hazy and it usually rains. It's like a rainforest, near the Lizard Motel. There's a pond surrounding the motel, and a swimming pool.
>
> Some guests leave, because they are afraid they'll disappear too.

The thunder strikes again, closer still, but the excited calmness remains; it's settled over us. I refold the paper, and put it back in its drawer.

The story all seems to occur in the present, but a present where everything that is here has always been and always will be, even the disappearances of the guests. Is the aura of the story cast in part by its grammar, by Dexter's use of verbs, seesawing between past and present?

Is this how children might envision death? That nothing

is ever truly lost, just gone, but will turn up somewhere else? The lizard, from his tilted head, appears to be watching me.

From beneath the leaf, I pick up the glass stopper, very carefully. "Dexter said that was the lizard's crystal ball," Clair whispers. It is even heavier than I remember: a heavy orb, wherein the world is twirled down to the inner eye of the glass. I see my face, and Clair's, in miniature. We wave to ourselves.

The days are grey. The branches are bare; there is mud, a battering of icy rain. We are counting down the days. My friend calls and invites me to go for a walk.

The woods are dreary. My friend is a cheerful sort, though; she is wearing a sweeping, midnight-blue coat, and walks at a brisk pace, and the coat swirls around her legs. She is wearing red lipstick. I take her lead and step resolutely through the dead leaves, as if we are actually going somewhere, instead of just meandering. She is a thoughtful, rather scholarly person who loves books, and in fact does volunteer reading once a week in an orphanage. We like to talk about books, and wonder together at the strange books assigned to our sons. Her son is twelve, like Alex, and also in the seventh grade.

"They've finished *Ransom*, about the kids being kidnapped," she tells me. She's heard that in a nearby town the seventh graders are reading *A Child Called It*, by David Pelzer, an adult memoir about a man's recollection of his childhood abuse. "What do you think?" she asks.

The dreary woods, and the idea of more abuse, and the pending events weigh on me, and I can't even muster a response. But she has enough energy for both of us. "I called a friend of mine who lives over there," she says, "and asked her how she feels about this. You know what she said? She said she looked at what the kids have been reading, and that she thought the books were good, because they were like a 'modern day *Oliver Twist*.'"

In the distance, for a moment, I see a deer, or at least a sense of deer, a white tail—sudden motion. It evaporates. I ponder what my friend has said. The hugeness of the difference between *Oliver Twist* and any of these books is too much to articulate. The whole of the nineteenth century in that book, the complexity, the subtlety, the vision of childhood. "For one thing," I hear myself say, "isn't *Oliver Twist* a great book?" And then I add, "What do real orphans like to read? Orphans who are eleven and twelve years old? Would you read them *They Cage the Animals at Night*, for example?"

She turns to look at me as we walk. "Oh my god no. They would hate it. It's too real. They would find it unbearable."

"They wouldn't take some comfort in it? What do they like instead?"

"You're not going to believe this," she says, and stops again. "And, no, they wouldn't take comfort in it. They like picture books. They like Dr. Seuss; they like *The Three Little Pigs*."

"You read twelve-year-olds *The Three Little Pigs?*" I try to picture this. "How did you hit on that idea? Aren't they seriously into being teenagers? Weren't you worried the first time you pulled the book out that they would feel insulted? And hate it?"

"Yes," she said. "The first time I was going to read, a girl who looked about eighteen (she was really maybe twelve), with long fingernails, kept tapping them on the table. It made me really nervous. But I had taken some of them to the library the week before, and what they gravitated toward was picture books, nursery rhymes in fact. These tough-looking kids were absolutely riveted by Mother Goose. It was really surprising. But I still worried the first time I decided to read—that that girl would hate it. But as soon as I started reading *Corduroy*—you know, about the stuffed bear who gets lost in a store—she stopped tapping her nails. She absolutely loved it. They all wanted me to read all the books over and over. That's what I do each week now."

So who are those sad books for? I wonder as we resume walking. Apparently, at any rate, not for real orphans.

❧ ❧ ❧

The morning of the surgery is grey, and in the pre-snow sky, the clouds seem low. The city is just waking as we drive down the highway; the streetlamps are still lit. Later, much later, Clair would tell us that she had been excited when we drove to her operation, that she had thought the operation would be "fun," as if we were giving her a party.

Her hair is in two braids for the surgery. She is given hospital pajamas, which are printed with circus bears. Everybody treats us politely. After a long wait, we are called, and Dan and I don the blue suits. It is cold in the pre-op room. Clair is allowed to ride in a toy jeep to the operating room.

A team of doctors and an anesthesiologist accompany us. Everyone is quiet, and we can hear the wheels on the jeep rolling. Only Clair is still somewhat jolly. Just as we come to the door of the operating room, Clair gets out of the car. As we are about to enter, she suddenly falls to her knees, grabbing the anesthesiologist, who is a sober German named Dr. Schmidt, and says, "You gotta help me, Doc! I'm doomed. I've got a wife and three kids at home!" Dr. Schmidt and the rest of us are bewildered, and frozen, for the moment. But then everyone bursts out laughing, Dr. Schmidt too. Clair stands up, and wipes her small hands on her knees. She shrugs and says, "I saw that on a Bugs Bunny cartoon once."

But in the operating room suddenly nothing is merry. Clair is shocked to find herself being lowered onto the steel table, to find herself strapped down, surrounded by machines. She begins to cry, and too late realizes she doesn't want to do this at all. Dan is stroking her hand, and I begin to sing to her, my singing voice as usual off-key, grabbing the first song I can think of, about a mother cow in a meadow. Dr. Schmidt slaps the mask over her face, muffling her cries. Now her eyes are rolling back, so that only the whites show, and she is being turned around. Dan and I are not wanted anymore, the doctors have taken over, and we are being ushered out, gently, but absolutely, and the metal door is shut behind us.

We just stand out there in the hall. We begin to walk. The hospital is an underground world of sick children and sleepwalking parents. I am aware of how my skin feels cold, and artificial, as if it is made of silly putty. Dan's hand is cold too. We walk. "What's that about the having a wife and three kids?" I say, and we laugh. Dan would like to go outside, buy a present for Clair, but I don't feel I can leave. It is going to be a long, long wait, but I want to stay near.

I am sitting tensely in the waiting room, amid other parents also waiting for their children to come out of surgery, when Dan pokes his head in and beckons me to the hall. "I got a stuffed animal," he says quietly from the doorway. "I don't feel right about bringing him in here for some reason."

The stuffed animal turns out to be a huge moose, nearly four feet high, with leather nostrils and thick furry antlers. I burst out laughing. This choice of a moose speaks of the kooky humor Dan and Clair share. The moose has a benign, pleasant face. His small eyes, made of glass, are close together, and his snout is bulbously large, managing to give him a pleasant yet slightly stupid look, as if he is bewildered by his own nose.

"This?" is all I can say.

"I thought she'd like him the best."

We stand with the moose out in the hall, since it does seem rude to bring him into the waiting room, where a silence hangs in the air. We watch all the people go by.

Doctors, nurses, wheelchairs. Families, here, in the middle of the day. Some people look up and smile at the moose. We stand under a clock, and the idea of the clock ticking asserts how much is going on right now, this very second.

⁂

Alex's voice sounds far away on the phone.

"Where are you?" he asks.

"We're still in the hospital and Clair is still having her operation, but she should be done pretty soon."

"You left her alone?"

"She's not alone, she's with the doctors. We can't go into the operating room."

He is quiet for a few moments. "Was she scared?"

"She was OK. She was a little scared, but mostly she was in a pretty good mood. She'll be fine."

"She's so lucky," he says after a while. "She gets all the attention."

"Well, it's not exactly that pleasant—"

"It doesn't hurt," he insists. "She'll say it hurts, but it doesn't."

Something explodes in me, and even though I know, somewhere, that he is speaking from fear and worry and mere childish rivalry, I sound belligerent when I demand, "How do you know?"

"If it was me getting an operation, I wouldn't be scared. I don't know why you're always making such a big fuss about it. It's just a little thing."

I want to say, "You stupid idiot! She's not lucky!" I think about thrusting him into the operating room, forcing him to see just how overwhelming the whole thing is, read him all the risk factors, make him watch her eyes rolling back—on and on. "How would you like to be strapped to a table?" I think of screaming.

I stop myself, remain mild, but I am left reeling.

It's good, of course, that I don't voice my rage. The next day, when we finally come home, we walk Clair slowly upstairs so she can lie down. She is still bandaged and drugged. Alex comes to me and whispers, "Are you going to go crazy?"

"Crazy? Of course not. What makes you think that?"

He shrugs.

He waits by Clair's room, and when she is awake enough, goes in to see her. Their voices are soft. I hear him say, "I was worried you would need me in your operation, and I wouldn't be able to help. I was worried you might need me."

I hear her say, "I was OK, Alex. I didn't need you. They took care of me."

When I walk by, I see that he is gently touching her bandage.

I am moved by this, and know that if I had voiced my rage, tried to stir up his guilt and worry, this would have interfered, not encouraged him to feel compassion. Again, I am glad I stopped myself.

But the impulse had been so intense. Why had I wanted so much to bypass his defenses, hold his face so he couldn't look away from suffering? What is the nature of this impulse? Rage at the survivor?

It's like the tone of some problem novels: the same bullying edge that assumes the reader has it easy and needs to be shaken out of his complacency.

Chapter Nine

Alex needs a new winter jacket. The one he's been wearing, which was originally a brighter blue, seems to have shrunk. I realize this on a cold morning, a few days after we are home from the hospital, when I suggest he zip up. He stares at me for a moment, and then rather theatrically pulls up the zipper, and instantly his whole body is forced in half, restricting his movements so he can only lumber around, his hands dangling, Frankenstein-like. But while I'm laughing, I feel bad: How could I have overlooked this?

The simple act of driving him shopping feels very good. In the glove compartment we find a heap of pink peppermints, which we both love. The day seems particularly bitter outside the car, but savoring the candy, turning on the heat vents, chatting, glancing at his profile, all the while barreling toward the prospect of a warm, new jacket—these things sharpen my senses; life is normal again. But lurking in the back of my mind is the uneasy thought that we never got around to finding him a new piano teacher. He's been without one since September, when we fired his old teacher, with whom he'd been working intensively for five years. While I am mulling this over, wondering how to remedy this quickly, I ask him, "Aren't you so glad the operation is over?" He shrugs. But when he excitedly adds, "It looks like it's going to snow," and I answer "Yes" (a bit more heartily than is warranted, since the sky is quite clear), I feel we are expressing how much we want things to just be normal and comfortable again.

Alex has always hated to shop, and this time is no different: a fast run in and out. He wants the first jacket he tries on, a shapeless, black thing, which I guess seems warm enough. I ask him if he's sure he doesn't want to try on any others, but he's sure, and carries the jacket in a ball to the cashier. We are back in the car so soon I am still sucking the same peppermint I went in with.

It is only the next morning that what had seemed uncomplicated skews slightly. When he tries the jacket on, studying himself in the mirror in the way he always does —fists at his hips, holding a deeply inhaled breath, his legs slightly apart like a superhero (I can almost make out a cape fluttering behind him)—he turns to me. "Does this look good?" he exhales. I study it. I have been gathering up old shoes piled on the porch, and am marveling at the sheer hugeness of an old black sneaker of his. The worn leather is textured with "air holes," as if some animal had once lived inside, and the shoelaces are so frayed that they have lost their entire original black casing, and have split open, revealing silky threads, that look like bright corn silk. While I am marveling, turning the shoe around in my hands, I am also wondering if in fact we *should* have bought the jacket in Medium instead of Large, since the jacket does, now that I look at it, seem too roomy, swinging at the hem as he moves. So I must have hesitated, because he goes on to say, "I mean it doesn't look, you know, too Columbine?"

"Like the school?" I say dumbly. "Where the shootings were?" But while I just begin to formulate questions (Did you think of this on your own? From watching TV, observing the dress of killers? Or is "Columbine" some new slang for—what?), he hugs me, in that new way he does—off-center, quick—and is out the door before I can ask him.

At 2:00 I have a mission, which is to lug Mr. Moose to Clair's classroom. He is heavy, since he is so large, and I decide to drive him over. Clair's teacher has designated 2:00 as the time Clair can tell the class about her operation, something she is looking forward to doing. Clair requested that I bring Mr. Moose over for the presentation, and that I attend too.

She leaps up to greet me. She has reserved a chair beside hers, in front of the room, for her moose. I am to sit in the back.

"Now you might wonder what an operation is," she says when she is sure she has everyone's full attention. "Well . . ." (A long dramatic pause; how did she get to be this master of ceremonies?) I survey the kids, who are all sitting cross-legged, slack-jawed, mesmerized, while Clair peers into their faces. "I" she points to herself, lest they be confused, "had one."

"Now," she goes on, "you can ask me questions." The children immediately raise their hands, and she points to each in turn.

"Did it hurt?"

"No, because they gave me some medicine."

"How come he's here?" pointing to Mr. Moose.

From where I sit, Mr. Moose looks slumped in his chair and appears to be nearly snoozing, his chin sunk in chest. But he is not without a certain humorous, watchful eye.

"My dad got him for me and he was in the hospital with me, and I just like him."

"Why did you get an operation?"

"I had a flap of skin growing in my ear."

"Did you get to keep the flap of skin?"

"No."

"Why not?"

"I didn't really want it."

"What did the doctors do?"

"They took out the skin."

"How?"

"I'm not sure, but they used some special tools."

"Like a hammer?"

"No some other tools they have in hospitals."

"Did they stick the tools in your ear?"

"Yes, I think so, but I was asleep when they did it, so I don't remember."

"Did you have dreams when you were asleep?"

"Yes, I dreamt about my mother."

Then everybody is raising their hands with questions, and she politely calls on each in their turn, and then everyone begins telling about a time they were in the hospital, or a time their grandmother died in a hospital, and then how they were born in the hospital, which begins to veer off into a discussion of getting hurt in general. Clair is patient, almost teacherly, as if she is giving a press conference.

It is only when someone asks, "Are you going to get to have more operations?" that I see her face darken, and if she were indeed a politician, this would be the moment when she'd say, "Interview Over," and duck the cameras.

⁂

The windshield is plastered with wet leaves. I am warmed by having been with Clair, by her bravery in front of her classmates, but she whispered to me when I left, "I'll miss you," even though, as I whispered back, I would see her at home in about fifteen minutes, since school was almost over. As I begin to drive, an image of her head bound in bandages comes to mind. Nonsensically I take solace in the fact that Mr. Moose has remained with her, since her teacher said he could "visit" for a few days.

Around the bend, a group of boys takes up the entire sidewalk, and I glide to a slow stop far enough away that they don't see me, but I can watch them for a few moments. Here are Alex and his friends. They are laughing, loose-limbed, leaping up to touch awnings as they pass, balancing on the curb, shoelaces untied. Around them, wet leaves are blowing, but they seem impervious to the wind; each is wearing a big, puffy jacket. Alex's jacket is no puffier than any others. His and all the others hang open, and a couple of boys have slung their jackets over their shoulders.

I have known all of these boys since they were little, but how, I wonder, might they look to someone who doesn't know them? Do they seem Columbine? Threatening, in some way?

They are moving so quickly, making so much noise, halting mid-march, their oversized jackets and huge pants ballooning out as they leap. Would someone find this energy, this potential, unsettling? For a moment it is as if I am watching them through water, as if they are a school of interchangeable fish; impossible to discern their outlines.

In fact, I remember as I watch, didn't I stand here with Alex, on this very corner, when he was four, watching a similar group of boisterous young teenage boys? We stood aside and let them pass. Where were they headed with such urgency? Alex was holding a huge plastic pink wristwatch we'd just bought at a stationery store, and he stood at attention, fascinated, slightly threatened. And later, come to think of it, I had overheard him playing with friends (these same boys that he's with now?); they'd come over for a play date, and spent the afternoon chasing bad guys. At some point I had casually asked, "So who are the bad guys?" and they told me, "The bad guys are teenagers!" They had been running around so hard they were sweaty, and we were having this conversation while they were gulping down juice. "But one day you'll be teenagers," I felt compelled to explain. Truthfully, though, did any of us believe me?

Where does this scary idea of teenagers come from? At the time, while the little boys resumed zooming around the house, tracking the wild, elusive teenager, I pondered this and remembered an article I'd read in college exploring adults' ideas about adolescence. Do these notions find their way into the writing of Young Adult fiction? "The adolescent has come to weigh oppressively on the American consciousness," I read. In fantasy, "he has invaded the adult world, in two antithetical stereotyped forms. In one he is the *victimizer,* leather-jacketed, cruel, sinister, and amoral, the carrier of society's sadistic and sexual projections, replacing the gangster and Negro in this role."

(The teenager is dangerous and unfeeling, and hence needs his books, like an ice-axe, to "break the frozen sea within"?)

And more: "In the other he is pictured as the *victim,* passive and powerless in the face of adult corruption that seeks to exploit his gullibility."

These ideas come back to me now, as I continue to watch the boys from the car. Suddenly the group comes to a halt. They have formed a cluster. When someone shifts slightly, I catch a glimpse within, and see none other than Alex, and get the quick impression he is doing some shtick, moving his hands expressively. But what about? I sit up, squinting. I see that he has furrowed his brow, in what I know to be mock fury, under which his blue eyes are blazing. For a moment he reminds me of a trout, colorful and glistening in sunlight, although just moments before, dull, submerged.

Then all at once an explosion of laughter, and the boys shoot backwards, clutching their sides. He alone is still standing, with a modest, happy look. When did he get so funny?

At home, Alex is starving, as usual. He takes off his jacket, and then hugs me hello. "Hi, Clair," he says. She is on the couch.

"Hi."

"How do you feel?"

"OK."

"How was school? Did you tell everyone about your operation?"

"Yeah. It was good. Everybody wanted to know if the doctor used hammers and those kind of tools to fix my ear."

He laughs. "What did you say?"

"I said he used other kinds of tools."

After they discuss this for a while, he comes into the kitchen, and he and I stand at the refrigerator. He is drinking orange juice. He looks up over the glass, and pauses. "Love you, Mom," he says. He goes back to drinking.

"Love you too, Alex. Did you have a good day?"

He evidences none of the high cheer or radiance that I glimpsed earlier. Instead, in a flat voice, he says, "Pretty good."

"I saw you with your friends," I venture. "They seemed to be laughing at one kid; was that kid cracking everybody up you?"

"Where were you?" he asks, lowering the juice, and looking levelly at me. "What did you hear?"

"Nothing. But I just saw you and it seemed like everyone was dying laughing. What in the world were you saying?"

He smiles slightly. "Just some stuff. I was just making some stuff up. When's Dad coming home?"

"Usual time." Then I add: "When you said 'Columbine' before, is that something you just thought, or do a lot of kids use that word?"

"Oh," he says, "I was just joking. I noticed on TV those boys wore big coats, for hiding weapons. It seemed like a good idea not to look like that."

"What's Columbine?" Clair calls.

"Nothing, Clair," he calls back. Then to me, in a quieter voice, he says, "All the kids keep wanting me to do impersonations of kids at school, but I don't feel too good about that. I don't want to be mean. I never know what to say when they ask."

We contemplate this: doing impersonations, however mild, does carry with it an implied mockery. I imagine getting impersonated, and how weird that might be. "You're right," I say. "Just turn the conversation away. I don't see any way to impersonate someone without making them feel self-conscious."

"But teachers are OK to imitate, right? I was doing impersonations of the teachers."

"Teachers seem better," I agree.

"What's Columbine?" Clair calls again.

On Saturday afternoon I stretch out on the living-room couch. My family is chatting in another room. It is a beautifully dreary day; we have been out all afternoon together, and now, at home, it feels like the perfect time of day to read. But I don't feel like getting up to find a book, and instead just lie here and look out of the window.

The day is dank. The only break in the grey landscape is a delicate strand of fairy lights strung through our neighbor's bush—the first holiday lights. The lights cause me to wonder, as I always do this time of year: How should we celebrate the holidays? We who are not members of a synagogue, who are not part of any organized religion? What should we celebrate? What should we buy for the kids? (There must be gifts.)

On a coffee table, beyond by my outstretched feet, is a brass samovar, plump, with a little spigot, and solid, shiny handles. It belonged to my grandmother, who had brought it over from Russia when she escaped. I am thinking of her now, while I study it, of a certain lushness to her presence, her scholarly looking spectacles. I used to lie on her couch, stretched out as I am now—she'd be cooking stew—and pretend I was a hobo, a grand, freewheeling hobo, whom she'd fussed over and who she insisted should lie down and relax. So there I'd lie. The house was fragrant. I can make out my feet in the brass, and remember how, back then, too, I used to study my reflection in the samovar's rosy surface, and marvel how I always seemed to be caught in the metal, as if I were a genie.

From the other room I can hear Dan's voice: he must have begun to tell a story to the kids. I can't hear the words, but his cadence reveals that this is his story-telling voice: brightly informative, as if he were a traveler who'd just arrived, who now, on a cold afternoon, lies by a roaring fire (we have no fire) and reports on the strange and largely wonderful things he came across while he was gone. His story is probably about "the puppy and the bunny," two characters he made up back when Alex and Clair were very small. The characters always happen to be in the midst of mishaps that mirror whatever mishaps might be unfolding at the moment in the kids' lives. If I strain to hear, I can make out certain words, or the thread of the story: "So they set out to try . . . find a contraption . . . the puppy needed." I hear the soft sound of a question by Clair, and Dan's bright response, something about "save the day."

The sun is beginning to sink. I get up, turn on a lamp, and glance at my family as I walk to the kitchen: Dan, whose high cheekbones and wide, dark eyes seem even more articulated than usual by the shadows of the lamp beside them. He is lying on the rug, against a wall, relaxed, his hands expressive. Alex is leaning against him, and Clair is sitting up attentively, hanging on every word.

What can I make for them? In the kitchen cabinet I find flour, sugar, vanilla. In the refrigerator, eggs, lemons. Butter. I take everything out. The story's shape is moving toward a happy ending, I can tell, and I think about what Bettelheim says a happy ending means to a child: "The prince and the princess getting married and inheriting the kingdom, ruling it in peace and happiness . . ." he wrote, "this is all the child desires for himself: to run his kingdom—his own life—successfully, peacefully, and to be happily united with the most desirable partner who will never leave him."

I pour the white flour in a hill, which is soft and cool. The vanilla beads on the top of the hill, and slides down the sides. It is relaxing to stir, to pour. The day calls out for a cake.

I mix ingredients for a while, grinding lemon rind so that the pith is extracted, and the air is pungent.

I have scraped the batter into a pan and put it in the oven. The oven is warm, and I lean against the belly of the oven.

I stay like that. I remember a warm light in a church basement: Adult Children of Alcoholics meetings. Rain against the windows, creaky wooden chairs. Tepid coffee in Styrofoam cups. I tended to keep a cup of coffee at the foot of my chair, untouched, but reassuring somehow.

I remember how we talked about our Inner Child. (None of us had our own children then; we were trying to "parent ourselves.") Told each other stories about our pasts: unhappiness, the mystery of survival. Terrible details. Cathartic. The children we spoke of had been huddled in the center of a sarcophagus; telling our stories was lighting a candle and calling, "Come out! You can come out!"

The lemon fragrance of the cake fills the kitchen, I am enjoying the warmth of the stove, and think how an adult remembering himself can be spry: can meld with the weak child in the dark; but then he can step out, too, and speak about him, from a distance. He knows that being a child isn't the whole story. Perspective gives you agility.

But what about a real child, living this moment in his actual childhood? Isn't his world largely foreground?

The cake is ready. My family has come out. I find some candles in a drawer, and on a whim I stick them in the cake and light them. We gather around the table. "What are we celebrating?" Clair asks. I hadn't thought of this aspect. "I guess we're celebrating that your operation is over," I say.

"Oh." She blows them out.

"Did you make a wish?"

"No, I can't since it's not my birthday." But a look of uncertainty crosses her face. "Can you make a wish if it's not your birthday?"

"Of course you can't," Alex says simply.

"Come on, Alex," Dan says. "What harm could it do?"

"Dad! You can't."

"He's right, Dad," Clair says.

We each take a slice, and begin to eat. The cake is warm. We watch the wind howling at the glass. After a while, Clair speaks in a small voice, almost to herself. "I used to think that when I blow out the candles, when it was my birthday, that's when I turn six, or seven, you know, my next age, but not before I blow." And then, pointing to wind swooping through the branches, she adds, "Look, the wind is changing its age."

"That makes sense," Alex says.

Do I vaguely remember thinking something like this too, long ago? For a moment I almost remember being a child, when there was a connection between candlelight and thresholds, when it was my own breath that seemed to cause the passing of a year.

Chapter Ten

"But we just did this," I hear myself say. And then, stupidly, "But it hasn't even snowed yet." After I say that, I am relieved to see the doctor isn't paying attention to me. He is looking at a calendar, choosing the new date for surgery. Clair's exam has revealed a problem. We will be going back into the hospital, not in the distant future, but now.

Where the first time was an ordeal, it was still manageable, but now I sense this was due largely to the fact that Clair had no frame of reference for what an operation was, didn't really understand what was involved. Now she does, and she wants no part of it. She is terrified.

Mostly her terror surfaces at bedtime. She is terrified to fall asleep. We take to having her sleep in bed with us, but we don't seem to offer much comfort: she remains ramrod straight between us. We try everything to comfort her. Dan sings to her, squelching his own anxiety to make a soothing lullaby, and for a few moments she calms down, and she dozes. But then she wakes up with a start. She wakes up crying, and because she is so exhausted and revved up from bad dreams, she is nearly hysterical. How do we comfort her?

"What are you afraid of?" I plead.

"My operation!"

"It will be OK. I will be with you the whole time."

"I'm so scared!"

"Of what? Of what are you afraid?"

"My operation!"

Then she breaks off, crying again. We switch the sleeping arrangements, Dan in her bed, she with me. We go over what will happen, how it wasn't so bad the last time, was it? How the operation is necessary, how eventually she will be able to have her hearing repaired. How Daddy and I will be with her the whole time. She lies still for a while, even drops off to sleep, but wakes, startled. Dan comes in and tries to tell her another bedtime story, beginning in his most soothing, protective voice, "Once there was a puppy who had to do something that was so scary. Did I tell you about that time?" And she wants to settle in, she lies in the crook of his arm, but a few minutes into it she crumples with tears again. "I can't pay attention," she whispers. This goes on.

The closest thing to a solution is one she comes up with: At bedtime she wants me to promise that I won't let her sleep past one hour, that once one hour is up, I'll immediately wake her up. This way, she reasons, she will have a guarantee that she'll be able to resume worrying. (I say OK, and in the morning I tell her I drifted off myself and therefore wasn't awake to wake her, but I promise I'll try harder the following night.)

Finally, as the week of the new surgery draws near, and we are all exhausted, I decide to take her to a psychiatrist. She wants me to stay in the session with her. I sit quietly nearby.

"Can you describe to me what you feel?" he asks.

She is small, sitting in what looks like a huge leather

chair. Will she be able to articulate anything? But a look of great seriousness has overtaken her face.

"That I will lose Mommy," she says. "That they put that thing over me to go to sleep." Then she adds in a little voice, "And I'm afraid I'll fade away."

He asks, "Are you afraid you'll die?"

I lurch in my seat. Shut up! I want to scream. Are you crazy? Why are you talking like that to my little girl? Why the hell are you speaking of death? She's only seven!

But she has brightened. "Yes," she is saying. "Yes! That's it exactly!"

I sit back, reeling, but say nothing. The room fogs out into a dream. The books, the couch, all look soft, far off. But their conversation continues. Their voices are calm.

"Everybody worries about that," he is saying. "You feel like you lose control. It's a scary feeling. I had surgery and I felt worried that I would die too. But you won't die. They are helping you to sleep—a deeper sleep than you would have on your own—so you won't feel pain, and they can take care of you. Then when they are finished taking care of you, they will bring you out of the sleep."

He has pulled out a medical book, and is showing her a picture of an ear, and the outer, middle, and inner canals. He is talking to her about the brain, about how the ear works. Clair loves science and is fascinated. She is standing next to him, with one hand on his shoulder, listening, asking questions, a little girl in a yellow dress. They are looking in the index together to see if they can find a picture of just the middle ear alone.

After the session is over, Clair sits in the waiting room

for a moment, and I go have a word with him. "I could never talk about that with her," I say. "About death. Are you sure it's a good idea? Won't it make her more scared?"

He says, "No, the opposite. It will make her more prepared." And he adds, "It is *your* fears that make it difficult to discuss it with her. It's too scary to *you*."

Afterward, Clair and I walk out to the car. It is night.

"I really loved that," she says. She stands with her hands clasped in front of her, and looks up at the stars. "I feel like a fog was lifted from my brain."

I am happy for her. But to me, the whole experience felt more dreamlike than anything I have ever experienced. While driving, Clair sits upright in the back seat, and I can see her in the rearview mirror. She is very alert, watching the road, her face lit by passing lights. Her expression is intensely thoughtful, as if truly she has been lifted from a fog.

How is it that facing the truth about reality, especially a harsh reality, causes such revitalization? Talking about fears of death and the facts of her soon-to-be operation has not burdened her, and in fact has lightened her load. Why is this so obviously helpful, while reality as presented in problem novels seems more often merely unsettling?

The answer, certainly in this case, is that the facts were revealed in the shelter of an adult presence; an adult clarified a scary reality that she alone has to face, and yet he, and I for that matter, were present. And didn't he take his cues from her? He didn't seem to be moving in with his own agenda, or his own timetable of when he thought she needed to know what, but in some sense she led the way.

Although he certainly didn't shy away from telling her the truth.

But the whole truth isn't always called for. I recall another moment when graphic depiction was not offered. "How do you get inside my ear?" she asked her surgeon once. He is a young surgeon, just starting out, a new father himself. He began to say something, but then seemed to think better of it. "Oh, I just have some special ways," he said. Then he waved a gentle furling of his fingers by her ear, like graceful tentacles underwater. It was a magical, pretty motion. Clair nodded, and smiled, since that was all she wanted to know.

Time is different in a hospital. Time is an infuriating block that doesn't budge, that refuses to be chipped away into minutes or hours. It certainly doesn't flow, certainly doesn't float you easily into late afternoon, so that you look up and wonder how it got so late. Maybe it's because you are hypervigilant while you wait, sitting bolt upright for six hours—but for what? You can do nothing. But you dare not let your attention veer. You sit like that under fluorescent lighting, breaking your vigil only to go to the bathroom. Time doesn't so much pass, in the hospital, as get lifted off your chest, and that only when the surgeon comes out, clearly exhausted, with the tumor in a jar, telling you your child is OK.

The night after surgery is flooded with relief, and now time does move, but the way a ship at night moves through ports and stops at villages where there is commotion and transactions, and the whole time you are only dimly aware of the noise and busyness, because you are so thin from exhaustion you can't even properly set the flat, vinyl mattress they gave you on the floor. Clair's IV makes a gurgling sound; she is lying in a cushy stupor. From the floor you can see her, her braids poking out either side of a bandage wrapped around her head: a girl soldier from the Civil War. Mr. Moose is sitting watch over her in a nearby chair. Once you wake up and imagine you see him smoking a cigarette, and think to yourself how risky it is to do this, in a hospital of all places.

After a while I give up trying to sleep. I stand. Clair smiles weakly at me. I am surprised to see it isn't even nine o'clock yet. I eat some Jell-O. I put a sheet on the mattress. I pull out my pajamas. I brush my teeth in the tiny bathroom, and the weariness shows in my face.

Before I lie down again I call home, and Alex answers. I am thrilled to hear his voice.

"How is Clair?" he says.

"She's doing OK. She's sleeping right now. She'll be fine."

"I know that. Of course she's OK."

"Well, she is. And I love you," I add.

"I love you too, Mom," he says. And then he says, "Mom," in a lower voice, one he reserves for the things that are very important, and I perk up as best I can, and squeeze into the chair beside Mr. Moose, prepared to listen.

"Mom, did you ever hear of Richard Pryor?"

"Richard Pryor?"

"I started listening to him," he says. "I got a tape. Dad said I could. He's so funny. He talks about crack. He talks from his life, it's very personal, but he makes it so funny."

"What are you reading for school?"

"Mom, I'll tell you another time. But I want to tell you about Richard Pryor. He's so funny. Is it OK with you? Dad said it was fine. He said it was art, so it was OK."

"What wouldn't I like about it?"

"It has cursing in it, that's all. Mom, he really is funny."

"Tell me."

"He's from the projects, did you ever hear of the projects? And I also started listening to Eddie Murphy's stand-up. They both grew up in the projects. But Eddie Murphy copies Richard Pryor. Eddie Murphy's father used to hit him, because he was a drunk; he's so funny when he's imitating his father. You'd like that part. But Richard Pryor is sweeter. He's the best. He can imitate animals so perfectly; and he tells what it's like to be on drugs, when he was hallucinating and when he blew himself up on crack. Did you know he did that? He almost died. But he was addicted. Now he says drugs are bad. And he talks about his father too. His stand-up is sad too, but it's the best. His timing is the best."

The truth is I am only half listening, and through my dopiness, drooped in the chair, the question I hear myself asking shows me that I've become obsessed with this: "Don't all those books you have to read in school deal with the same issues, like being beaten by fathers and alcoholism? What's different?"

He is incredulous. "Mom, you don't understand! This is comedy! It's funny! There is nothing the same! They are the opposite!"

⁂

The long night begins. Clair sleeps. The nurses change shifts.

I venture out for a little walk. There are no windows along the hall, everything is turned inward, and this fact reminds me of Las Vegas: it could be any time. It could be the middle of the afternoon, but for the fact that the rhythm has slowed; a few lights are dimmed; nothing seems as acute. No visitors burst through the doors. I am so tired I feel as if I am already sleeping, and my legs are drained of feeling. But the prospect of that noisy room and flat mattress keeps me walking.

I wish I could call Dan. I wish this more than anything. I wish we could hold each other. I wish I could hear his voice. But it's too late to call. I wish I could climb into a bed here.

"Can I help you?" A nurse's voice startles me. She is smiling helpfully in the doorway. She is a very blonde woman, with high color, not in the least tired, not clued in to the fact that it is the middle of the night. Her coloring and good cheer suggest someone who has been out on a picnic at noon.

"I am looking for a soda machine," I hear myself say.

"Oh, on the seventh floor." And then adds brightly, "It's great up there! You'll love it. They just finished it." She talks as if we are in France and she is making a suggestion for a neat sightseeing excursion. With a flip of her hair she is on her way.

In the elevator I am a woman among a gaggle of male doctors, and I studiously look ahead, with an affected, haughty stare; but we all stare straight ahead, into our reflection in the elevator doors: a herd of gleaming doctors and one exhausted woman in pajamas. When the doors open on seven, and I am the only one to step out, I do so with my head high.

And out into a vast, quiet world. What floor is this? The air feels suddenly different—purer—like air in the country. And here, extending fifty feet, along an entire wall, an enormous mural, appearing to be a photograph of night. Of buoyant children in space suits floating though the starry depths of night.

I stand before it. Being greeted by this just off the elevator, swallowed up by it really, has the effect of being told, in silent eloquence, "It is different here," and "This is another planet."

Where am I? I walk the glorious length of the photograph. There is a feeling of moonlight. The floating children look intent, happy, and I am reminded of the joyful abandon of jumping on a trampoline, of the way swimming felt when I was a child. Close up, I notice that the children are tethered by thin filaments, only faintly indicated, to some unseen spacecraft, so their safe return is ensured. Looking closer still, I see that their space suits faintly resemble blue scrubs doctors wear in the operating room, and the children's helmets can also almost look like bandages. This must be the intensive care unit. The filaments, while looking like lifelines, are also IV's, which of course are lifelines of a sort. But this is only faintly suggested. This photograph is full of suggestions.

I like it here. The shiny floor gives way to miles of soft green carpet. Quiet. No bustle like downstairs. No dingy white linoleum. Along the sides of the vast room, soft-looking couches, and on each, curled in deep sleep, exhausted parents. The children must be in rooms beyond. Radiators hiss along the walls. It is warm.

I sink into a little couch of my own. The couch is voluptuous, coral-colored. I lean back and prop my feet on a small orange ottoman. What thoughtful artist considered how to design an intensive care unit and make it . . . happy? And interesting?

Next to me is a window, and I can see the night city, watchful, twinkling. I sit for a while, the emotions of the day draining away. I doze. The children continue to float happily across the huge midnight wall. Once or twice I open my eyes and glimpse hidden dimensions in the photograph. The reality of illness is present. "The sickest children," it whispers, "must be tethered from floating away forever. We will do whatever we can to keep them."

But their tenuousness is expressed not by visions of passive, frightened children hanging on by a thread; instead, these weightless children are brave explorers in a huge moonlit frontier. Even the idea of death is present, in the hugeness, the depth, of the night sky. But if death comes, the wall seems to say, the heavens are not empty. There are other children there. There is lightness. And we on earth can watch them, as they watch over us.

I doze again, aware always of the floating photograph. How is it that through a metaphor you can glimpse the deepest and scariest reality, and not feel despair? How is it that knowing one thing through the mirror of another is more restful, and more apt, than viewing that one thing alone?

After a while I get up to head back to Clair. I feel a bit refreshed. At the end of a hall, I see the soda machine, which looks sleek, framed in chrome. I slip the coins into the slot, and after much clatter, a can clonks down, as if I've hit the jackpot. The soda is icy cold. I am so thirsty, and this quenches my thirst.

It began to snow on our way to *The Producers,* softly in a vague sky, and collected around poles and on cars, just a few drifting flakes.

Inside the theater, we forgot about the snow, slung our damp coats over our seats, and when the lights went down and the show began, we forgot about everything else. Clair sat propped on a phone book. Alex laughed so much that a man and wife sitting in front of us, who had not laughed at all, turned to him at intermission and scolded him to stop making such a racket. The husband was a red-faced boar, and the wife, who seemed to me someone used to interpreting her husband to the world, said, "You're giving my husband a headache with all your noise."

I panicked. Shouldn't I say something? While I was fretting over what to do, Dan leaned over to suggest they move their seats, since laughing is what we've come to do.

And thankfully, the couple did move to other seats during the intermission. And I was surprised, thrilled, that their comments didn't seem to affect Alex: he just kept on cracking up. He knows this world, I thought, this palace of Mel's, of humor, of the theater. He was radiant sitting next to me, alive, electric. This, I thought, this is his unit.

When we came out, it was into a world transformed, muted and buried, thick snow still falling steadily. The city through the snow was softly glowing. We walked happily to the car, Clair skipping, Alex chatting about the play, and then breaking into song, "Springtime for Hitler . . . and Germany!" although his voice was hard to discern, since the wind had picked up. While we walked, we marveled at the fact that what had started as a few frail flakes, hardly convincing, had accumulated so quickly.

It continues to snow the next day. I am standing on my porch, drinking a cup of coffee. The windows resist the wind as it tugs at them, but they do not open, since we finally fixed their latches—not an easy task. The hardware was old and corroded, and had to be gouged out and replaced. Now it is warmer in here. And since the windows aren't flying open, I can regard them, and admire the frames Alex painted last summer, soft grey with hopeful yellow lights made with that tiny brush, and the pink daisies Clair painted along the ledge. I watch the snow steadily through the glass. It has filled up the yard, covering the crab apple tree. The white fence is barely visible.

Clair runs up the walk, rosy and happy. She has at least one more operation in her future, but this won't be for a year, so we are, at the moment, free. She has been playing with her friends Abe and Dina across the street. "Hi, Mommy," she says when she bursts in, and hands me a package.

"What's this?"

"Abe's mom gave it to me for you."

There is a note taped to the outside of the package, which I unfold. "Hi. I know you love these books," my sarcastic friend has written, "so I thought this one might be especially interesting. We got it as a gift. It has everything you want in a kid's book—incest, therapist-patient sex, and of course domestic violence that leads to murder. It says on the back that it's meant for kids twelve and up, so obviously it's appropriate for Alex. Pass it on with my love."

I stand frozen, lost in thought, until Clair speaks.

"What's in the package?" she says.

"A book. Do you have homework?"

"Yeah. But I want to play first."

"You were just playing all afternoon! What homework do you have?"

"Oh, we have to write something."

"What?"

"Oh, just something. But you know what? Abe and Dina said they want to make *London's Deepest,* definitely."

What exactly is *London's Deepest* about? I wonder. She is taking off her boots, and I intend to ask her what this entails. But for the moment I slip the book out of the envelope.

"What is it?" Alex calls from the couch. He has apparently been watching through the window, and listening.

Clair takes the book from me. She is very proud of how she can read. She sounds out the words. "*When Dad Killed Mom*, by Julian Lester," she says proudly.

"Just some book," I say. Then I slip it back in its envelope, until I can read it later in private. Or not.

POSTSCRIPT:
What Does He Need to Take with Him?

"Would he have the patience to study some music theory?" the jazz musician asked me over the phone.

"I'm not sure," I said, "but probably."

"Well, bring him in, and we'll see. And if he wants to bring some music he's worked on, that would be good. I want to see how he approaches the piano."

On that first visit Alex was trepidatious, but the idea of jazz appealed to him. The musician turned out to be a man in his sixties, calmly welcoming us into his small tidy apartment in the Bronx. I sensed he was a shy man, and Alex stood shyly next to me. I left them alone, and when I returned an hour later, I was surprised to see them both happy, and Alex eager to make the next appointment. The teacher told us to buy the *New Real Book*.

Later, we took Alex to hear his teacher perform in a club. His teacher was a genuine artist: the moment he touched the piano, it seemed as if he was resuming playing, simply re-entering a whole musical world that he'd momentarily stepped out of. The music flowed out of him. Alex sat upright, clearly riveted, not moving for the entire set. After this, not without anxiety, Alex resumed practicing, something he had spent many hours doing in the past. Once, I overheard Alex telling Clair that his teacher lived in a kind of "castle." The lessons have continued ever since.

Today, I sit in his teacher's kitchen; it is too cold to walk around for the hour. There is a bit of an old-world formality to their relationship, in that once we've arrived, they get right down to work, the door closed. The carpets muffle their sounds, but I can hear through the walls that Alex is playing "Satin Doll." The tones are not quite as swanky as they will be, yet the fluency of the music is moving, like hearing Alex alone, how his uninterrupted voice away from me will sound.

So I sit quietly in the tidy kitchen and listen, and wonder, as I often do: What does a young person need from his family and culture, when he is about to set out on his own? I take notice of the potholder hanging neatly over the stove on a little hook, and the gleaming spice rack. A small jade plant on the windowsill is healthy. A well-ordered existence. What does a knight setting forth need to carry in his sack?

Alex is happy when he comes out. His teacher tells me he is going to Japan for two weeks but will call when he returns. They nod goodbye to each other, and smile. If Alex were older, perhaps they might shake hands. Alex and I walk to the car.

"Did you have a good lesson?"

"Yeah. It was great."

"What was so good about it?"

"It was fun."

"How is it different from your old lessons?"

"It just is."

We climb into the car, and begin to drive. "He was chewing gum," Alex says. "He was so proud of his gum." He imitates his teacher chewing, sitting close to him and watching, all the time chewing thoughtfully, humming, slightly off-key. I think, not for the first time, how Alex has an uncanny ability to capture someone—a gist, an essence. In the imitation is great affection. Alex is beaming, chewing, thinking about his lesson.

After a while he says, "He doesn't call the jazz songs 'music,' he calls them 'tunes.'"

"Did he give you tunes to practice while he was away?"

"Yeah, here, he wrote it down."

I glance over and see scribbles in pencil. It has started to snow again, and I need to watch the road. "I can't read while I'm driving."

"All the songs he gave me have sort of the same titles." He reads the note out loud:

> There will never be another you
> All the things you are
> The song is you

We watch the snow. I put the heat on. "They all have sort of the same titles," he repeats. After a moment he adds, "What if these weren't the names of songs, but they were just little messages he wants me to have, since he's going away? Like how he felt about me?"

I think about this—how that is good, the feeling that no matter how far you go, you are loved, you remain connected; art links you. Is this what should be in the sack? How do you put a feeling in a sack?

He is imitating his teacher's slight drawl: "Alex, my boy, There'll never be another you, because of All the things you are. Yes sir, my boy, The song is you." The snow falls, and the car is warm. We laugh.

Notes and Further Thoughts

Epigraph: Edith Cobb, "The Ecology of Imagination in Childhood," *Daedalus* 88 (1959): 538–539.

Chapter One

p. 3: *world of grownups* Pablo Neruda, *Memoirs* (London: Penguin Books, 1977), 20.

Chapter Two

p. 18: *in vision and strength* Katherine Paterson, *Bridge to Terabithia* (New York: Harper Collins, 1977), 126.

p. 25: *from another world* Gaston Bachelard, *Poetics of Reverie: Childhood, Language, and the Cosmos* (Boston: Beacon Press, 1971), 114.

p. 30: *let you exist in it* Georges Poulet, "The Phenomenology of Reading," in *Contemporary Literary Criticism*, ed. R. C. Davis (New York and London: Longman's, 1986), 351.

Chapter Three

p. 35: *problems in their own lives* C. Huck, S. Hepler, J. Hickman, B. Ziefer, eds., *Children's Literature in the Elementary School* (Madison, Wis.: Brown and Benchmark, 1997), 455.

p. 36: *for a breath of air* Alfred Kazin, *A Walker in the City* (New York: Harcourt, Brace and World, Inc., 1951), 8.

p. 39: *adolescent's inner feelings* Anne Scott Macleod, "The Journey Inward: Adolescent Literature in America, 1945–1995," in *Reflections of Change: Children's Literature since 1945*, ed. Sandra L. Beckett (Westport, Conn.: Greenwood Press, 1997), 125.

p. 39: *The Catcher in the Rye* Regarding *The Catcher in the Rye* as the prototype for the first problem novels, see Anne Scott Macleod, ibid., 126; also Gail Schmunk Murray, *American Children's Literature and the Construction of Childhood* (New York and London: Twayne Publishers, 1998), 185.

p. 39–40: *came the Deluge* Anne Scott Macleod, *American Childhood: Essays on Children's Literature of the Nineteenth and Twentieth Centuries* (Athens, Ga.: University of Georgia Press, 1994), 199.

p. 40: *child defined by the terminology of pain* Sheila Egoff, *Thursday's Child: Trends and Patterns in Contemporary Children's Literature* (Chicago: American Library Association, 1981), 67, 14.

p. 40–41: *some of its characteristics* For a description of the problem novel, see Egoff, 67.

p. 41: *What You See Is All There Is* Roderick McGillis, "Terror Is Her Constant Companion: The Cult of Fear in Recent Books for Teenagers," in *Reflections of Change: Children's Literature since 1945*, ed. Sandra L. Beckett, 102–103. Reviewing problem novels that have fear at their core, McGillis writes: "These books reflect a society numbed to the very forces that erode safety and community. Speaking of family, these books depict a world in which no one has a family, no one has security. . . . Darkness has truly drawn down; the center has completely fallen apart" (104).

p. 43: *and virtually all problem novels* While books such as *The Man in the Ceiling* by Jules Feiffer, *Johnny's in the Basement* by Louis Sachar, *The Kid in the Red Jacket* by Barbara Park, or *The Education of Robert Nifkin* by Daniel Pinkwater might deal with real-life problems, it is precisely the fact that they operate within a slightly magical dimension, expressed not so much by manifest magical happenings as by the nature of the humor and the oftentimes kooky logic of the narrative voice, that distinguishes these from what I understand problem novels to be. In these books the narrator depicts a universe that doesn't quite adhere to average laws, but swerves whimsically from expected conventions. *Johnny's in the Basement*, for example, a story about a boy (Johnny Laxatayl) having to forgo a childhood hobby of bottle cap collecting, but more largely about leaving childhood behind and beginning to grow up—a serious theme indeed—begins: "When Johnny was nine he received a letter from the President of the United States. It read: 'Dear Johnny, I heard about your bottle cap collection. I'm glad to be able to do my share. Yours truly, the President.' Along with the letter came a ginger ale bottle cap. It was bent in the middle from when the President had pried it off with his bottle opener. Johnny threw the letter away and tossed the bottle cap in with his other ones" (New York: Avon Books, 1981). This book, and others like it, seem to suggest that a (wacky) world exists in tandem with the everyday world, and has influence over the latter. There is rarely any levity in a problem novel, whereas in the aforementioned book, and others like it, levity abounds.

p. 44: *to work or home* Paula Fox, *Monkey Island* (New York: Dell Yearling, Random House Children's Books, 1991), 60–61.

p. 45: *as about a terrible situation* I do not mean to suggest that all juvenile books about children in dire situations, about children facing adversity, need to be looked at in the same critical light. Certainly, there are many wonderful books that address complex, "real" material. It is not so much a book's content (although this is important too) that I am addressing here, as the way the content is handled. Perhaps what is most problematic in certain books I discuss is what can be called a "problem novel lens": a lens that seeks to see the child as primarily alone, as struggling to survive, unimaginative, connected to no meaningful community. Looking at a story about troubled family life, for example, through this lens usually reduces the story, so that no matter how interesting the plot, how rich the language, the story is remembered and experienced primarily by its feeling state, which is generally hopeless, and is characterized by the characters' and perhaps the author's sense of the need for diminished expectations in life (some would say realistic expectations). Where this narrow lens is widened, stories are free to develop more richly. The material can breathe. A story that addresses a child in a difficult family situation (mother dead, father gone off to war) but that is not told through this particular lens is *Lily's Crossing* by Patricia Reilly Giff (New York: Dell Yearling, 1997). In this book, a fuller portrait of a child is offered. *One More River*, by Lynne Reid Banks (New York: Avon Books, 1973),a book about a girl growing up during the Six Day War, also handles difficult material beyond the narrowing "problem novel" lens.

p. 45: *rob somebody and kill some people* Mark Twain, *Huckleberry Finn* (New York: New American Library, 1997), 17.

p. 46: *seem not to regard play in this way* The fact that a depiction of violent play would not be found in a modern Young Adult novel underlines the drastic fall from grace that the imagination has suffered in popular understanding. There is a fundamental belief, it seems, that to pretend in a fantasy is tantamount, or too close, to doing that thing in reality—that fantasy, like behavior in civil society, thus ought to be kept to the straight and narrow. But isn't the reverse more true: that playing, where fantasy is encoded in games, in scenes, or as Huizinga writes, in "a temporarily real world of its own . . . expressly hedged off for it," might actually diminish the likelihood that such fantasies will break through into real life? (Johan Huizinga, *Homo Ludens: A Study of the Play Element in Culture* [Boston: Beacon Press, 1950], 14.)

p. 46: *soon get over it* Mark Twain, *Huckleberry Finn,* 44.

p. 47: *Zinnia Taylor: explorer* Sharon Creech, *Chasing Redbird* (New York: Harper Trophy, 1997), 25–26.

p. 48: *all tangled up in one pot* Creech, ibid., 1–2, 5.

p. 49: *an adult disguised as a child* A more extreme version of an adult-created child, who has little or no imagination, is the child so often portrayed in TV sitcoms and in some current movies. The children I am thinking of are wisecracking, world-weary, sensible, literal—sometimes seeming more like disillusioned middle-aged adults than children. On such shows, the adults, conversely, are like overgrown, goofy kids. The role reversals are extreme. In fact, it is easy to imagine that the concocted child, were he to encounter a "real" child, would find the latter annoying.

p. 51: *about real children* Gail Schmunk Murray, *American Children's Literature and the Construction of Childhood,* Introduction.

p. 52: *remained highly idealized* Murray, ibid., 145, 146–147.

p. 52: *kindness toward children* Anne Scott Macleod, *American Childhood: Essays on Children's Literature of the Nineteenth and Twentieth Centuries,* 169.

p. 54: *fetch more breakfast* Ian Serraillier, *The Silver Sword* (New York: Criterion Books, 1959), 120–121.

Chapter Four

p. 59: *The realm of childhood* Gail Schmunk Murray, *American Children's Literature and the Construction of Childhood,* 185–186.

p. 59: *the world flowed in* Anne Scott Macleod, *American Childhood: Essays on Children's Literature of the Nineteenth and Twentieth Centuries,* 65.

p. 60: *any type of discussion* Paul Zindel, *The Pigman* (New York: Bantam Books, 1968), 57–58.

p. 60–61: *even though he's dead* Zindel, 86–87.

p. 61: *numbness of being lonely* Jacket copy, *The Pigman.*

p. 62: *no place to hide* Zindel, 49.

p. 62: *cherish for life* Jean Little, "A Writer's Social Responsibility," in C. Huck, S. Hepler, J. Hickman, B. Ziefer, eds., *Children's Literature in the Elementary School,* 459.

p. 65: *Official Knowledge* This phrase occurs in Michael W. Apple, *Cultural Politics and Education* (New York and London: Teacher's College Press, 1996), Introduction.

p. 66: *seeing the canyon* Walker Percy, "The Loss of the Creature," in *The Message in the Bottle: How Queer Man Is, How Queer Language Is, and What One Has to Do with the Other* (New York: Farrar, Straus and Giroux, 1975), 48.

Chapter Five

p. 68–69: *starry night trembled cold* Juan Ramón Jiménez, *Platero and I,* trans. Eloise Roach, (Austin: University of Texas Press, 1957), 158.

p. 70: *Life's longing for itself* Kahlil Gibran, *The Prophet* (New York: Alfred A. Knopf, 1923), 17.

p. 80: *as if they were one organism* Anna Freud and Sophie Dann, "An Experiment in Group Upbringing," in *Psychoanalytic Studies of the Child* (New York: Summit Books, 1951), 6:127–168.

p. 88–89: *the open destiny of life* Grace Paley, "Conversations with My Father," in *Enormous Changes at the Last Minute* (New York: Farrar, Straus and Giroux, 1974), 161–162.

Chapter Six

p. 105: *one finds on the dump* Wallace Stevens, "The Man on the

Dump," in *The Palm at the End of the Mind: Selected Poems and a Play,* ed. Holly Stevens (New York: Vintage, 1967), 163–164.

p. 105: *to discover a self* Edith Cobb, "The Ecology of Imagination in Childhood," 540.

p. 109: *that they themselves have access to magic* On the child's interest in seeking buried treasure, see Selma Fraiberg, "Tales of the Discovery of the Secret Treasure" in *Selected Writings of Selma Fraiberg,* Louis Fraiberg, ed. (Columbus: Ohio State University Press, 1987).

p. 109: *with hardly any effort* Vladimir Nabokov, *Conclusive Evidence* (New York: Harper & Brothers, 1951), 6–7. Nabokov describes his early creative life this way: "I may be inordinately fond of my earliest impressions, but then I have reason to be grateful to them. They led the way to a veritable Eden of visual and tactile sensations. One night, during a trip abroad, in the fall of 1903, I recall kneeling on my (flattish) pillow at the window of a sleeping car (probably on the long-extinct Mediterranean Train de Luxe, the one whose six cars had the lower part of their body painted in umber and the panels in cream) and seeing with an inexplicable pang, a handful of fabulous lights that beckoned to me from a distant hillside, and then slipped into a pocket of black velvet: diamonds that I later gave away to my characters to alleviate the burden of my wealth. I had probably managed to undo and push up the tight tooled blind at the head of my berth, and my heels were cold, but I still kept kneeling and peering. *Nothing is sweeter or stranger than to ponder those first thrills. They belong to the harmonious world of a perfect childhood and, as such, possess a naturally plastic form in one's memory, which can be set down with hardly any effort; it is only starting with the recollections of one's adolescence that Mnemosyne begins to get choosy and crabbed"* (my emphasis).

p. 110: *create everything for himself* But what is the connection between the urge to create and the orphan fantasy? (Obviously one can feel the desire to create without the presence of this fantasy; I am wondering, however, about the particular nature of the creative impulse within the orphan fantasy.) The orphan fantasy, as I have observed it played out in Story Shop, and as I remember it from my own childhood, seems accompanied by a huge desire to discover and make things, and the child's belief, however unconscious, that just about anything—human beings, water, electricity—is within his power to create, or to otherwise stumble upon its origins. The orphan feels the need or desire to make *everything*—to create the world from scratch.

Consider children's desire to make "potions"—an activity that seems to be loved at about seven or eight and to go on to a greater or lesser degree throughout middle childhood. So certain was I (at about age eight or so) for example, that I would eventually hit upon the right formula to concoct a real person—all I had to do was keep trying out different ingredients together: mud, rainwater, toothpaste, salt, and stick it all into the freezer—so certain was I of my eventual success, that when I checked on the progress of my experiments in the freezer, I often opened the door very cautiously, in case this was the day that I'd find a very tiny girl, pink from cold, having just come alive. She would be rubbing her eyes, sitting on the edge of the ice tray.

Perhaps at this juncture it is most interesting to speculate that such early alchemy, and the orphan's desire and power to make everything and anything, can be thought about in light of how Mircea Eliade discusses primitive man's need for sacred space: "Territory," he writes, "can be made ours only by creating it anew." (Mircea Eliade, *The Sacred and The Profane: The Nature of Religion,* translated from the French by Willard R. Trask [San Diego: Harcourt, Inc., 1987], 32.) Could it be that the orphan, like primitive man, sets about creating his universe, so that he can make it his own?

p. 115: *before being there to be found* D. W. Winnicott, "Communicating and Not Communicating Leading to a Study of Certain Opposites," in *The Maturational Processes and the Facilitating Environment: Studies in the Theory of Emotional Development* (Madison, Conn.: International Universities Press, Inc., 1965), 190. The passage in which this occurs reads: "At adolescence when the individual is undergoing pubertal changes and is not quite ready to become one of the adult community there is a strengthening of the defenses against being found, that is to say being found before being there to be found. That which is truly personal and which feels real must be defended at all cost, and even if this means a temporary blindness to the value of compromise. Adolescents form aggregates rather than groups, and by looking alike they emphasize the essential loneliness of each individual."

p. 119: *the sea frozen inside us* From a letter written by Franz Kafka to Oskar Pollak, Jan. 24, 1904, printed in *Franz Kafka: Letters to Friends, Family, and Editors* (New York: Schocken Books Inc., 1977), 16. This reference, and its relation to problem novels, came to my attention through a discussion by Anne Scott Macleod in *American Childhood: Essays on Children's Literature of the Nineteenth and Twentieth Centu-*

ries, 196–197. Macleod suggests that the Young Adult author Robert Cormier's novels echo Kafka's sentiment. She quotes Kafka more fully: "If the book we are reading does not wake us, as with a fist hammering on our skull, why then do we read it? Good God, we would also be happy if we had not books, and such books as make us happy we could, if need be, write ourselves. But what we must have are those books which come upon us like ill-fortune, and distress us deeply, like the death of one we love better than ourselves, like suicide. A book must be an ice-axe to break the sea frozen inside us."

Chapter Seven

p. 122: *woken up... writerly* Lucy McCormick Calkins, "Rehearsal: Living the Writerly Life," Chapter 3 in *The Art of Teaching Writing* (Portsmouth, N.H.: Heinemann, 1986). The idea of writerly-ness, and being wide awake, however, run through all her work as central ideas.

p. 123: *never miss a day* Lucy McCormick Calkins, *Raising Lifelong Learners: A Parent's Guide* (Reading, Mass.: Addison-Wesley, 1997), 170–171.

p. 123: *there in their lives* Calkins, 80.

p. 124: *your writing talent* Calkins, ibid., 78–79.

p. 125: *non sequiturs* Calkins, ibid., 25.

p. 126: *Does my life really matter?* Calkins, *The Art of Teaching Writing*, 15–16.

p. 130: *the façade of a castle* Alfred Kazin, *A Walker in the City*, 17.

Chapter Eight

p. 149: *actual sentiments of these persons* Erskine Caldwell and Margaret Bourke-White, *You Have Seen Their Faces* (New York: Viking Press, 1937). The quote appears in the book's disclaimer.

Chapter Nine

p. 170: *exploit his gullibility* E. James Anthony, "The Reactions of Parents to Adolescents and to Their Behavior," in *Parenthood, Its Psychology and Psychopathology,* ed. E. James Anthony, M.D. (Boston: Little Brown and Company, 1970), 309.

p. 174: *will never leave him* Bruno Bettelheim, *The Uses of Enchantment: The Meaning and Importance of Fairy Tales* (New York: Vintage Books, 1989), 147.

p. 175: *largely foreground* Do problem novels spring in part from the adult's impulse—as he remembers difficulties from his own childhood long ago—to offer help to a child as the adult wishes he had been helped? Is there an implicit fantasy on the part of the adult (the adult writer, reader, public) that in giving a child a book about suffering in childhood, that one can, through identification with the child, call back across time, into one's own childhood, and reassure "You are not alone" and "You will survive!"

This impulse is understandable and humane. And yet it seems important to make a distinction between one's "inner child," that is, the child in an adult's memory, and an actual child. An adult remembering his childhood has the benefit of a broad perspective, whereas an actual child, whose brain is developing, whom time hasn't delivered very far, can't possibly have these same powers of perspective. How could a child who hasn't passed through adolescence yet, or hasn't yet completed it—who hasn't emerged—possibly have the same context for understanding experience as an adult?

It seems crucial to consider that the stories we imagine we would have needed then, the ones we imagine might have comforted us, and explained the difficulties we were living through, cannot—simply cannot—have the same meaning to an actual child who is at this very moment in his childhood.

Acknowledgments

I wish to thank the following people: I am indebted to Kim Larsen, roommate of yesteryear, and Christiane Bird, wonderful, complex writers both, and careful, generous readers. We have been a writing group for nearly twenty years, and the group has been a creative mainstay for me. Thanks to my dear writing and walking pal Penny Wolfson—mile after mile we've trod, incubating, hatching plots, stopping to eat those huge sandwiches. I am indebted also to Susan Vunderink, smart, generous, fun friend and insightful critic; to my pal Meryl Schneider, whose aesthetic sense—particularly where the color turquoise is concerned—and warm compassion nourish me. Heartfelt thanks to Noelle Oxenhandler, teacher and friend, whose writing inspired me long before we met. Also to Roger Sutton, for answering questions about some current trends in children's literature. To my readers: Jenny Dellaverson, Dr. Sylvia Lester, Iris Hisky Arno, Anne Marie McIntyre, Mia de Bethune, and Richard Lewis—I am deeply grateful for your feedback and support. Thanks go also to Dr. Barry L. Singer, Ilja Wachs, and to Karen Weinstock and Linda Azif, both of whom inspired my children to love to read and write. Thanks to my agent Ellen Levine and her able assistant Melissa Flashman. To Joanne Wyckoff, my editor at Beacon Press—who knew (I didn't) that having an editor could be so interesting and illuminating?

Special thanks to the delightful children of Story Shop and their families, and in particular thanks to Julia Pilowsky for allowing me to excerpt "Millenius Shack"; Ben van Buren for his description of what Gertrude imagined; and Dexter Dine for "Lizard Motel."

To two teachers: My great thanks and appreciation to Mrs. Marianne Lester, my brilliant teacher at Sarah Lawrence College, who alerted me, in the most interesting ways possible, to the connection between poetry and psychology. And to Lawrence Weschler, without whose insight, questions, encouragement, and fabulous "Fiction of non-Fiction" class I might not have quite written this book, and certainly would not have had the gumption to get up and try to publish it. To Ren I owe more than I can express.

To my family—my parents and brother David, and to my children, I am enriched by love from all. To Dan, my beloved lifelong partner, who has been supportive throughout, is an astute critic, and provides an endless source of inspiration, I express my gratitude.